CONTENTS

INTRODUCTION

CrossTrain Your Brain is a brain-exercise program designed by experts in the field. It works on the proven principle that mental muscle, much like physical muscle, can be gained and maintained through an exercise regimen. The program parallels a physical workout routine at your gym. These exercises bring novelty and new intriguing mental challenges and are designed to help you build a better brain. The workouts are anything but routine, boring, or time-consuming. In fact, they are structured as games and puzzles to ensure fun and enjoyment. Broken into three parts; left brain (verbal), right brain (visual, spatial), and whole-brain (right-left intuitive thinking), some exercises are stress free while others are more challenging. Just as a sedentary lifestyle won't keep your body in peak physical condition, a sedentary brain won't retain its mental edge. Retaining peak mental performance is the key to reversing the mental deficits associated with an aging brain, including memory loss, sluggish thinking, and problem-solving confusion.

Before you get started, it's interesting to know which side of your brain is dominant. Brain dominance relates to specific mental functions and thinking styles. Most people have a preferred brain-dominance orientation. Your brain dominance will create an affinity for and ease with some puzzles over others. If you are left-brain dominant, you'll definitely enjoy the word games, and if you are right-brain dominant, you'll enjoy the visual puzzles. You may even be tempted to stick with the exercises that match your brain dominance and skip those that do not. But that would defeat the purpose of a cross-training program, and your gains would be minimized. Remember, the more a mental workout takes you out of your comfort zone, the more novelty it brings to your brain. And the greatest gains come with novelty, because new brain pathways are being created.

CROSSTRAIN YOUR BRAIN

HUNDREDS OF PUZZLES AND EXERCISES THAT PROVIDE THE ULTIMATE CRANIUM WORKOUT

CORINNE L. GEDIMAN

SELLERS
PUBLISHING

DEDICATION

To the memory of Harry Lille

— *Corinne L. Gediman*

Published by Sellers Publishing, Inc.
Copyright © 2019 Sellers Publishing Inc.
Text and puzzles copyright © 2019 Corinne L. Gediman
All rights reserved.

Sellers Publishing, Inc.
161 John Roberts Road, South Portland, Maine 04106
Visit our Web site: www.sellerspublishing.com
E-mail: rsp@rsvp.com

ISBN 13: 978-1-4162-4671-8

Managing Editor: Mary L. Baldwin
Production: Charlotte Cromwell
Designed by George Corsillo/Design Monsters

10 9 8 7 6 5 4 3 2 1

Printed and bound in the United States of America.

LEFT-BRAIN CHARACTERISTICS

The left side of the brain excels at language skills, verbal processing, sequential reasoning, and analytical thinking. Individuals who favor this type of thinking are said to be left-brain dominant. They are characterized as logical and rational thinkers capable of excelling in many fields. When problem solving, left-brain dominant thinkers arrive at the solution or big picture by analyzing and organizing the step-by-step details along the way. They are good forward planners and usually enjoy "talking out" a problem. Some fields that attract a left-brain person are science, mathematics, writing, accounting, financial services, teaching, medicine, engineering, research, library science, and computer programming.

RIGHT-BRAIN CHARACTERISTICS

The right side of the brain excels in visual-spatial reasoning, random processing (i.e., free association), intuition, perceptual organization, and holistic thinking. Holistic thinkers are able to "see" the "whole" as a picture. They retain information through the use of images and patterns. Perceptual organization, a right-brain-dominant strength, is the process by which the brain takes bits and pieces of visual information (colors, lines, shapes) and structures the individual parts into larger units and interrelationships. Individuals who excel in perceptual organization show an ability to arrange color, lines, and shapes into creative works of art, sculpture, and architecture. Some occupations that attract a right-brain person are inventor, architect, forest ranger, illustrator, artist, actor, athlete, interior decorator, beautician, mathematician, computer-graphics designer, craftsperson, photographer, recreation director, marketing designer, retail specialist, yoga/dance instructor, art director, web site designer, fashion designer, and product-package designer.

ARE YOU RIGHT OR LEFT BRAIN?

The Brain-Dominance Self-Assessment below will provide insight into whether you are naturally left-brain or right-brain dominant. It will help you understand where your mental strengths lie, as well as what your greatest "mental stretch" opportunities are.

For each item, circle the letter "a" or "b" beside the answer that most closely describes your preference. You must choose either "a" or "b" — you cannot choose both. If you are not sure, consider what your response would be if you were in a stressful, difficult, or new situation. We tend to revert to our natural brain dominance when under pressure.

1 I am often late getting places.
 a. yes
 b. no

2 When you are learning dance steps, it is easier for you to . . .
 a. learn by imitation and by getting the feel of the music.
 b. learn the sequence of movements and talk yourself through it.

3 If I don't know which way to turn, I usually let my emotions lead me.
 a. yes
 b. no

4 Can you tell approximately how much time has passed without a watch?
 a. yes
 b. no

5 I find that sticking to a schedule is boring.
 a. yes
 b. no

6 If I lost something, I would visualize where I last saw it.
 a. yes
 b. no

7 Setting goals for myself helps me to keep from slacking off.
 a. yes
 b. no

8 When I work, I tend to . . .
 a. focus on one task at a time.
 b. multitask; have a bunch of projects going at the same time.

9 I feel most comfortable when there is a specific set of directions to follow.

      a. yes
      b. no

10 Does the expression "Life is just a bowl of cherries" make sense to you?

      a. yes
      b. no

11 I am musically inclined.

      a. yes
      b. no

12 My desk, work area, or laundry room is . . .

      a. cluttered with things I might need later.
      b. organized and neat.

13 Do you sometimes act spontaneously or come to premature conclusions?

      a. yes
      b. no

14 Some people think I'm psychic.

      a. yes
      b. no

15 When I need to learn how to use a new piece of equipment . . .

      a. I jump right in and wing it.
      b. I carefully read the instruction manual before beginning.

16 Are you a romantic dreamer or a logical planner?

      a. romantic dreamer
      b. logical planner

17 Before I take a stand on an issue, I get all the facts.

      a. yes
      b. no

18 I like to draw.
   a. yes
   b. no *(circled)*

19 I lose track of time easily.
   a. yes *(circled)*
   b. no

20 I feel comfortable expressing myself with words.
   a. yes *(circled)*
   b. no

21 If you forget someone's name, would you go through the alphabet until you remembered it?
   a. yes *(circled)*
   b. no

22 Have you considered being a poet, a politician, an architect, or a dancer?
   a. yes
   b. no *(circled)*

23 Have you considered becoming a lawyer, a journalist, or a doctor?
   a. yes
   b. no *(circled)*

24 I keep a "to do" list.
   a. yes *(circled)*
   b. no

25 Is it easy for you to categorize and put away files?
   a. yes *(circled)*
   b. no

Answer Key

If your answers to the questions above are fairly evenly distributed between left- and right-brain responses, you are a "whole brain" thinker with the flexibility to draw on the strengths of both brain hemispheres. If the majority of your responses fall into one or the other brain-hemisphere categories, your natural tendencies are to draw on the strengths of your primary brain dominance as you engage in everyday activities and challenges.

15

Left-Brain Responses: 1. b, 2. b, 3. b, 4. a, 5. b, 6. b, 7. a, 8. a, 9. a, 10. b, 11. b, 12. b, 13. b, 14. b, 15. b, 16. b, 17. a, 18. b, 19. b, 20. b, 21. a, 22. b, 23. a, 24. a, 25. a

10

Right-Brain Responses: 1. a, 2. a, 3. a, 4. b, 5. a, 6. a, 7. b, 8. b, 9. b, 10. a, 11. a, 12. a, 13. a, 14. a, 15. a, 16. a, 17. b, 18. a, 19. a, 20. a, 21. b, 22. a, 23. b, 24. b, 25. b

GETTING STARTED

You are now ready to begin your journey toward becoming a brain athlete! Remember that the key is to relax and have fun. Did you know that stress kills brain cells? So no stressing. You are about to do something really good for yourself. Enjoy it and feel proud.

LEFT BRAIN

CAN YOU SAY IT?

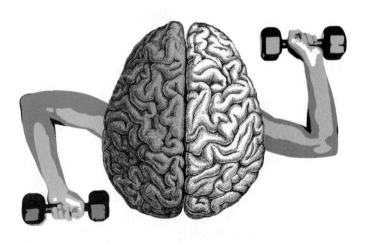

VERBAL EXERCISES

LEFT BRAIN: CAN YOU SAY IT? VERBAL EXERCISES

INTRODUCTION:
The focus of the left-brain exercises is on the left hemisphere's natural proclivity for language skills. Keeping language processing sharp as we age is critical to memory formation, storage, and retrieval. In this left-brain workout, you will participate in a variety of entertaining verbal exercises.

LEFT   RIGHT

Logic
Analysis
Sequencing
Linear Reasoning
Mathematics
Language
Facts
Thinking in Words
Words of Songs
Computation

ANIMAL ANALOGIES

HOW TO PLAY: In its simplest form, an analogy is a stated likeness between two sets of things that are otherwise unlike. To solve the missing analogy, your first step is to determine the relationship between the first two italicized words. You must then complete the second pairing so it has a parallel relationship. In the example below, the relationship is about characteristics of each species.

Bird is to *fly* as *fish* is to: <u>swim</u>

A characteristic of a *bird* is its ability to *fly*, while a parallel characteristic of a *fish* is its ability to *swim*.

See how quickly you pull up the correct response for each of the missing analogies below.

1. *Wasp* is to *sting* as *snake* is to <u>bite</u>.
2. *Dog* is to *bark* as *donkey* is to <u>hee haw</u>
3. *Duck* is to *webbed* as *horse* is to <u>hoove</u>.
4. *Snake* is to *reptile* as *frog* is to <u>amphibian</u>
5. *Salmon* is to *fish* as *dolphin* is to _____.
6. *Duck* is to *duckling* as *cow* is to <u>calf</u>.
7. *Lizard* is to *vertebrate* as *cricket* is to _____.
8. *Leopard* is to *carnivore* as *giraffe* is to _____.
9. *Dove* is to *white* as *canary* is to <u>yellow</u>.
10. *Zebra* is to *stripes* as *leopard* is to _____.
11. *Polar bear* is to *Antarctica* as *panda* is to _____.
12. *Fish* is to *gill* as *rabbit* is to _____.
13. *Mosquito* is to *six legs* as *spider* is to _____.
14. *Goose* is to *flock* as *buffalo* is to _____.
15. *Cockatoo* is to *feathers* as *camel* is to _____.

Left Brain: *Can you say it?* 13

ANSWER KEY

ANIMAL ANALOGIES

1. bite
2. bray
3. hoofed
4. amphibian
5. mammal
6. calf
7. invertebrate
8. herbivore
9. yellow
10. spots
11. Asia
12. lung
13. eight legs
14. herd
15. hair

COLOR CONUNDRUM

HOW TO PLAY: The names of colors are often combined with everyday words to form new words. In this game, you will be presented with a palette of color words and a set of noncolor words. Your brain challenge is to form compound words by combining a color word with a noncolor word. The color word can come before or after the noncolor word. For example, if the noncolor word "out" is preceded by the color word "brown" it forms the compound word "brownout," referring to a period of reduced electrical voltage. See if you can create at least 50 compound words by combining the color and noncolor words.

COLOR PALETTE

blue, black, brown, gold, green, pink, purple, red, white, yellow

NONCOLOR WORDS

nose	out	jacket	carpet	code	law	fool's
house	cross	blood	digger	neck	print	lie
mail	ball	fever	jack	grass	bellied	bird
dust	board	cap	sheep	smith	coat	list
fish	bell	heart	lily	eye	thumb	horn
hot	rush	coast	peace	market	true	solid
moon	herring	tape	bread	rule		

ANSWER KEY

COLOR CONUNDRUM

Here are 50 answers and there are many more. Can you find them?

1. BLUE: bluebell, bluebird, blue blood, code blue, bluegrass, blue law, blue moon, blueprint, true blue

2. BLACK: blackball, blackcap, blackjack, blacklist, blackmail, black market, blackout, black sheep, blacksmith

3. BROWN: brownnose, brownout

4. GOLD: Gold Coast, gold digger, gold dust, goldfish, fool's gold, solid gold, Golden Rule, gold rush

5. GREEN: greenhorn, Greenpeace, green thumb

6. PINK: pinkeye, hot pink

7. PURPLE: Purple Heart

8. RED: red carpet, redcoat, Red Cross, red herring, red-hot, redneck, red tape

9. WHITE: whiteboard, white-bread, whitecap, White House, white lie, lily-white

8. YELLOW: yellow fever, yellow jacket, yellow-bellied

WORD IMPOSTERS

HOW TO PLAY: You will be presented with a list of words. Some are spelled correctly, and some are spelled incorrectly. See how quickly you can find the spelling errors and correct them. Circle the misspelled words, then write the correct spelling in the box to the right. There is a total of four misspelled words.

Review all of the words, one at a time.

1. acquaintance	
2. Caribbean	
3. indispensible	
4. questionaire	
5. rhythm	
6. inngenius	
7. hypocrisy	
8. ukelelee	
9. dumbell	
10. coliseum	

ANSWER KEY

WORD IMPOSTERS

4. questionnaire
6. ingenious
8. ukulele
9. dumbbell

HARRY POTTERISMS

HOW TO PLAY: J. K. Rowling's Harry Potter series captured the hearts of young and old around the world. It also spawned a vocabulary of its own. See if you can remember or guess the meaning of the words below, from the fanciful world of Muggles and wizards.

LEARNING THE SPELLS

Potterisms	English Translation
1. Floo powder	
2. Charm School	
3. Deathday party	
4. Disapparate	
5. Half-blood	
6. Firebolt	
7. Muggle	
8. Parseltongue	
9. Quidditch	
10. Remembrall	

ANSWER KEY

HARRY POTTERISMS Learning the Spells

1. powder you throw into the fire, to go wherever you want
2. class at Hogwarts in which you learn about useful spells and charms
3. ghost birthday party
4. leave a place by apparition
5. a person with Muggle and wizard ancestors
6. fastest broomstick model
7. a nonmagical person
8. language spoken by snakes
9. a sport in which wizards fly on brooms
10. a small, glass ball that has smoke inside that turns red when you forget something

WORD KNITTING

HOW TO PLAY: In this game, you are challenged to combine 20 divided words into 20 whole words by matching the front and back halves of each word together. The words are not necessarily divided by syllable. For example, when you match "TRIU" with "MPH," they combine to make TRIUMPH. Cross off your matches as you go along.

CARS

NIS	SA	US	OTA	VOL
BU	PEU	OLDS	INFI	FO
VO	AC	SU	BISHI	AT
SLER	FI	CHRY	AU	MER
LEX	TOY	CEDES	SAN	NITI
GUAR	RD	HON	JA	LIN
BARU	MITSU	COLN	DI	URA
MOBILE	DA	GEOT	TURN	ICK

ANSWER KEY

WORD KNITTING Cars

Acura, Audi, Buick, Chrysler, Fiat, Ford, Honda, Infiniti, Jaguar, Lexus, Lincoln, Mercedes, Mitsubishi, Nissan, Oldsmobile, Peugeot, Saturn, Subaru, Toyota, Volvo

BIRDS OF A FEATHER

HOW TO PLAY: In the English language there exists a multitude of words that mean *group*, and the words can differ depending on the makeup of the group. In this mix-and-match game, your brain challenge is to match a specific group of animals with its collective name. Draw a line to make a match.

ANIMALS	COLLECTIVE NAME
1. antelope	a. sleuth
2. bass	b. clowder
3. bacterium	c. gloat
4. bear	d. paddling
5. cat	e. herd
6. caterpillar	f. skulk
7. clam	g. shoal
8. crocodile	h. army
9. duck	i. culture
10. fox	j. bed

ANSWER KEY

BIRDS OF A FEATHER Animals: A–F

1. e
2. g
3. i
4. a
5. b
6. h
7. j
8. c
9. d
10. f

OPPOSING PROVERBS

HOW TO PLAY: Proverbs are expressions that capture the wisdom of the ages in pithy phrases. Yet when examined closely, some proverbs actually offer contradictory points of view. For example, the proverb "A silent man is a wise one" seems to be contradictory to "A man without words is a man without thoughts."

To play, match the number of the proverb on the left to the letter of the contradictory proverb on the right. Write the letter of the opposing proverbs in the spaces indicated in the left column.

1. Knowledge is power. __	a. Too many cooks spoil the broth.
2. Look before you leap. __	b. Out of sight, out of mind.
3. Beware of Greeks bearing gifts. __	c. If you want something done right, do it yourself.
4. With age comes wisdom. __	d. The more things change, the more they stay the same.
5. Nothing ventured, nothing gained. __	e. Life is what you make of it.
6. Money talks. __	f. Fools seldom differ.
7. Great minds think alike. __	g. Ignorance is bliss.
8. Birds of a feather flock together. __	h. He who hesitates is lost.
9. Many hands make light work. __	i. The best things come in small packages.
10. Two heads are better than one. __	j. Better safe than sorry.
11. The only constant is change. __	k. Talk is cheap.
12. The bigger the better. __	l. Opposites attract.
13. Absence makes the heart grow fonder. __	m. Forewarned is forearmed.
14. What will be, will be. __	n. Out of the mouths of babes, come wise words.
15. Cross your bridges when you come to them. __	o. Don't look a gift horse in the mouth.

ANSWER KEY

OPPOSING PROVERBS

1. g
2. h
3. o
4. n
5. j
6. k
7. f
8. l
9. a
10. c
11. d
12. i
13. b
14. e
15. m

TOM SWIFTIES

How to Play: Tom Swifties are puns. A *pun* is a form of wordplay that suggests two or more meanings, by exploiting multiple meanings of words, or of similar-sounding words, for an intended humorous or rhetorical effect. Look at the following example sentence: "I believe there are 527,986 bees in the swarm!" Tom recounted.

The play is on the verb "recounted," which has a double meaning. It means both numerical counting and narrating a set of facts. It is the double meaning that creates the humorous effect.

In this game, you will be presented with a series of Tom Swifty sentences. Each sentence contains a scrambled pun. Your challenge is to unscramble the scrambled puns in italics.

TAKE IT EASY
In this round, take all the time you want. You can even ask a friend for help.

1. "I need an injection for the pain," Tom pleaded in *n i v a*.

2. "It's the maid's night off," said Tom *l y l e s s p l e h*.

3. "I have a split personality," said Tom, being *r n k f a*.

4. "I'm just an ordinary solider," Tom admitted *l y v a t p e r i*.

5. "I'm losing my hair," Tom *l w d e b a*.

6. "I'll never give up my hounds," said Tom *e d l y g g o d*.

7. "I am waiting to see the doctor," said Tom *t n a p e i t y l*.

8. "We have no bananas," said Tom *r u f i y l e s s l t*.

9. "I will drive you to the emergency room," said Tom *a s i p t o h b y l*.

10. "I'm halfway up the mountain," Tom *g a l l e e d*.

Answer Key

TOM SWIFTIES Take It Easy

1. vain
2. helplessly
3. frank
4. privately
5. bawled
6. doggedly
7. patiently
8. fruitlessly
9. hospitably
10. alleged

SYNONYM PRETENDERS

HOW TO PLAY: In this game, you must decide which of two choices is the synonym of the key word and which is the pretender. Circle the choice you feel is the real synonym.

1. Intently
a. resolutely
b. irresolutely

2. Piteous
a. painful
b. sorrowful

3. Relentlessly
a. adamantly
b. pushily

4. Garish
a. colorful
b. tawdry

5. Hypocritical
a. phony
b. judgmental

6. Repulsive
a. smelly
b. offensive

7. Primly
a. scornfully
b. formally

8. Liberated
a. rescued
b. opened

9. Contemptible
a. vile
b. untrustworthy

10. Theory
a. speculation
b. thought

11. Fortitude
a. endurance
b. fearlessness

12. Sporadic
a. periodic
b. unconnected

13. Muddled
a. entangled
b. addled

14. Flank
a. center
b. edge

15. Dumbfounded
a. confused
b. speechless

ANSWER KEY

SYNONYM PRETENDERS

1. a
2. b
3. a
4. b
5. a
6. b
7. b
8. a
9. a
10. a
11. a
12. a
13. b
14. b
15. b

WORD MULTIPLIER

HOW TO PLAY: You will be presented with a grid containing letters that make up a common word. Your challenge is to mix and match the letters to make as many new words as possible. Each new word should contain four or more letters. Vowels can be used more than once in the same new word. You will be playing against a computer program that generated new words, based on the letters in each grid. How many new words can you come up with? See if you can match or beat the computer!

CREAM

C		R
	E	
A		M

NEW WORDS:

BREAD

B		R
	E	
A		D

NEW WORDS:

ANSWER KEY

WORD MULTIPLIER

Cream

acme, acre, mace, race, came, ream, care, cram, mare

Bread

abed, bare, dare, dear, bade, bead, bard, bear, bred, drab, read, brad

PIRATE LINGO

HOW TO PLAY: *Pirates of the Caribbean*, starring Johnny Depp, unleashed a passionate interest in "pirates" across a wide gamut of moviegoers. In this game, you will be presented with "pirate lingo." Your challenge is to guess the meaning of each of the pirate expressions. Even if you don't have a clue, use your imagination and make up a meaning. Who knows, you might be right!

SETTING SAIL

Pirate Lingo	Meaning
1. Fly the Yellow Jack	
2. Give no quarter	
3. Shiver me timbers	
4. Dance with Jack Ketch	
5. A taste of the cat	
6. Crack Jenny's teacup	
7. Parlay	
8. Avast	
9. Cackle fruit	
10. Take a caulk	

ANSWER KEY

PIRATE LINGO Setting Sail

1. illness aboard
2. show no mercy
3. expression of surprise
4. hang
5. whipping
6. spend the night in a house of ill repute
7. pirate code of conduct; discussion between disputing parties
8. stop
9. hen's eggs
10. nap

COMMON SAYINGS

HOW TO PLAY: In this game, you must find the two words — one from the first column, one from the second column — that, if combined, could lead to a common expression, and then write the phrase in the third column below. Use each word only once. For example, the words "ace" and "hole," if combined, could lead to the common expression "ace in the hole."

EASY TIMES   **COMMON EXPRESSIONS**

puppy	music
baker's	test
monkey	wood
apple	buck
diamond	bucket
face	love
kick	dozen
knock	business
nest	down
pass	eye
dumb	egg
acid	rough

ANSWER KEY

COMMON SAYINGS Easy Times

1. puppy love
2. baker's dozen
3. monkey business
4. apple of my eye
5. diamond in the rough
6. face the music
7. kick the bucket
8. knock wood
9. nest egg
10. pass the buck
11. dumb down
12. acid test

WORD BOGGLER

HOW TO PLAY: In this game, you will be presented with a matrix filled with letters. The objective is to form words by connecting adjacent letters. Letters that are above, below, to the left or right, or on a diagonal to each other are all acceptable connections. For each set, you will be given one free word clue. See how quickly you can find the free word. Play against a friend to see who can find the most words. Or see how many words you can find in two minutes.

FREE WORD CLUE: WHAT HAPPENS WHEN YOUR CAR BREAKS DOWN ON THE ROAD?

C	R	U	L
A	K	P	S
G	T	W	E
B	O	H	D

FREE WORD-CLUE ANSWER:

OTHER WORDS:

ANSWER KEY

WORD BOGGLER

Free Word Clue: What happens when your car breaks down on the road?

Free Word-Clue Answer: towed

Other words:

six letters: slurped, pulsed, carped

five letters: slurp, pulse, depth, carps, tarps, swept

four letters: wept, used, tows, toga, tarp, tack, swot, swob, spur, spew, sped, slur, ruse, rack plus, pews, owed, lurk, hews, carp, bows, both

three letters: who, wed, use, ups, two, tow, tog, the, tar, tag, sew, rat, rag, pus, pew, owe, how, hot, hog, got, dew, cat, car, bow, bog, ark arc, ago

OXYMORONS

HOW TO PLAY: An oxymoron is a figure of speech in which two words that contradict each other are used together. An example would be "jumbo shrimp." When we put "jumbo" (large) and "shrimp" (small) together, it opposes common sense, but it is nonetheless an accurate description of a kind of crustacean. An oxymoron is a mini-paradox.

In this game, you will connect words from Column A with words from Column B to form common oxymoron phrases.

COLUMN A

1. freezer
2. speed
3. science
4. random
5. constant
6. act
7. virtual
8. benevolent
9. spend
10. modern

COLUMN B

a. order
b. thrift
c. naturally
d. history
e. despot
f. burn
g. fiction
h. change
i. limit
j. reality

Answer Key

OXYMORONS

1. f
2. i
3. g
4. a
5. h
6. c
7. j
8. e
9. b
10. d

TWISTED PROVERBS

HOW TO PLAY: In this game, you will be given half a traditional proverb, with an improbable ending. Your challenge is to guess the correct ending of the proverb.

1. It is always darkest before . . . daylight savings time.

2. Never underestimate the power of . . . nature.

3. It is better to light one small candle . . . than to waste electricity.

4. A rolling stone . . . could crush you.

5. I think, therefore I . . . get a headache.

6. Early to bed and early to rise . . . is the first in the bathroom.

7. A journey of a thousand miles begins with a . . . blister.

8. The grass is always greener . . . when you leave the sprinkler on.

9. Don't count your chickens . . . it takes too long.

10. Where there's smoke there's . . . pollution.

11. A penny saved is . . . a slow road to retirement.

12. Strike while the . . . match is hot.

13. The squeaky wheel . . . gets on your nerves.

14. If you lie down with dogs . . . you'll smell bad when you get up.

15. If you can't stand the heat . . . don't light the fireplace.

ANSWER KEY

TWISTED PROVERBS

1. the dawn
2. human stupidity
3. than to curse the darkness
4. gathers no moss
5. am
6. makes a man healthy, wealthy, and wise
7. single step
8. on the other side
9. before they're hatched
10. fire
11. a penny earned
12. iron is hot
13. gets the oil
14. you'll get up with fleas
15. get out of the kitchen

HIPPIE LINGO

HOW TO PLAY: The "hippie" youth movement began in the mid-1960s in the United States and soon spread to countries around the world. Hippies were countercultural pacifists who advocated "making love not war." Often referred to as "flower children," they sometimes lived in communes and were often characterized by long hair, psychedelic rock music, love beads, sexual liberation, and drug use that helped them to achieve altered states of consciousness. They also evolved their own unique and colorful language.

In this exercise, you will be presented with a series of Hippie Terms. Your challenge is to provide the common English definition of each term.

Hippie Terms	Meaning
1. "crash pad"	
2. "What's your bag?"	
3. "Can you dig it?"	
4. "a gas"	
5. "split"	
6. "scene"	
7. "pigs"	
8. "groovy"	
9. "tripping"	
10. "far out"	
11. "selling out"	
12. "threads"	
13. "hang loose"	
14. "flaky"	

ANSWER KEY

HIPPIE LINGO

1. a place to sleep it off
2. What's your thing; what are you into?
3. Do you get it?
4. a blast, a good time
5. leave; depart
6. a happening
7. derogatory term for the police
8. fun, enjoyable
9. having a hallucinogenic experience from drugs
10. taking things to the limit
11. giving in to traditional social-establishment values
12. clothes
13. Take it easy; don't get uptight.
14. ditzy

MIXED-UP ANALOGIES

HOW TO PLAY: In its simplest form, an analogy is a stated likeness between two things that are otherwise unlike. In solving an analogy, your first step is to determine the relationship between the first two italicized words. You must then select words for the second pairing that have a parallel relationship. In the example below, the relationship is about characteristics of each species:

A characteristic of a *bird* is its ability to *fly*, while a parallel characteristic of a *fish* its ability to *swim*.

TAKE IT EASY

1. *Dime* is to *ten* as *half* is to _____.

2. *Football* is to *helmet* as *soccer* is to _____.

3. *Rabbit* is to *hole* as *lion* is to _____.

4. *Down* is to *up* as *red* is to _____.

5. *Cell phone* is to *battery* as *television* is to _____.

6. *Road* is to *car* as *air* is to _____.

7. *Bring* is to *brought* as *go* is to _____.

8. *Conductor* is to *orchestra* as *coach* is to _____.

9. *Crab* is to *crustacean* as *mouse* is to _____.

10. *Seventy* is to *69* as *eight* is to _____.

ANSWER KEY

MIXED-UP ANALOGIES Take It Easy

1. 50
2. shin guard
3. den
4. green
5. electricity
6. airplane
7. went
8. team
9. mammal
10. seven

COMMON SAYINGS

HOW TO PLAY: In this game, you must find the two words — one from the first column, one from the second column — that, if combined, could lead to a common expression. For example, the words "ace" and "hole," if combined, could lead to the common expression "ace in the hole."

FUN TIMES

COMMON EXPRESSIONS

creek	thumb
pig	sleeve
fly	paddle
drop	kite
wolf	ointment
fly	clam
roll	bucket
rule	sheep
happy	poke
nothing	punches

ANSWER KEY

COMMON SAYINGS Fun Times

1. up a creek without a paddle
2. pig in a poke
3. nothing up my sleeve
4. fly in the ointment
5. drop in the bucket
6. wolf in sheep's clothing
7. go fly a kite
8. roll with the punches
9. rule of thumb
10. happy as a clam

HOMONYMS

HOW TO PLAY: Homonyms are often used to create a witty "play on words," (e.g., there's a rabbit breeder who combs his *hare* every morning). They are words that sound exactly or almost exactly the same, have different meanings, and are spelled differently. You will be presented with a sentence that is missing two words. Fill in the blanks with the two homonyms that will make a logical sentence. For example, *It's a _____ idea to try to _____ yourself a glass of milk with your eyes closed.* The two homonyms that would make a sensible sentence are *poor* and *pour*.

COLORFUL PHRASES

1. My father recently _____ *The Hunt for* _____ *October.*

2. The toy boat with the red _____ was on _____.

3. When I spilled the cake _____, every _____ in the vase turned white.

4. I _____ out my birthday candles, even though it made me _____ in the face.

5. The _____ _____ a mistake and cleaned the coffee table with brown shoe polish.

ANSWER KEY

HOMONYMS Colorful Phrases

1. read, *Red*
2. sail, sale
3. flour, flower
4. blew, blue
5. maid, made

FILM STARS

HOW TO PLAY: In this puzzle, you must find the last name of a famous film star hidden in a sentence about him or her. Here is an example:

"He stood _ TALL_ _ _ when he played Rocky Balboa."

Who is the famous actor hidden in the sentence?

Add letters to form a name. That's right — Sylvester Stallone.

WHAT IS THE NAME OF THE ACTOR HIDDEN IN EACH SENTENCE?

1. He played a B _ A _ D_ guy in *The Godfather*.

2. Her fans went to S _ _ EE _ her in *Julie & Julia*.

3. He owned a B _ _ A R _ in *Casablanca*.

4. He had a famous movie _ C _ _ A R _ E _ E _ _ _ R before he became a state governor.

5. The hills A _ _ R E _ _ alive with the sound of her music.

6. He _ _ C _ _ A N claim credit for the evil character of Lex Luthor in the *Superman* films.

7. The ladies swoon when watching this sexy dance star S W A Y _ _ to the music in films like *Dirty Dancing*.

8. She _ _ R A N _ _ _ away with her best friend in the movie *Thelma and Louise*.

9. This movie star appeared in _ O N _ _ *Golden Pond* with his real-life daughter.

10. This glamorous blonde actress was _ O N _ _ _ President Kennedy's top-ten guest list while he was in the White House.

ANSWER KEY

FILM STARS What Is the Name of the Actor Hidden in Each Sentence?

1. Brando

2. Streep

3. Bogart

4. Schwarzenegger

5. Andrews

6. Hackman

7. Swayze

8. Sarandon

9. Fonda

10. Monroe

HETERONYMS

AT WORK

1. The computer *console* is taking up too much space on my desk.

   Alternative definition of heteronym: _____

2. The in-focus machine *projects* the image from your computer onto the screen.

   Alternative definition of heteronym: _____

3. Her boss told her that her *conduct* in the meeting was unacceptable.

   Alternative definition of heteronym: _____

4. The college student was hired as an *intern* for the summer.

   Alternative definition of heteronym: _____

5. The interviewer was impressed with her business *resume*.

   Alternative definition of heteronym: _____

ANSWER KEY

HETERONYMS At Work

1. comfort
2. plans
3. lead
4. confine
5. start over

CRAZY CONSONANTS: X, J & K

HOW TO PLAY: Certain consonants, like l and r, are in many words and other consonants are in far fewer words. Maybe because they're pretty rare, words with x, j, and k seem to have funny and memorable sounds. It's hard not to love words like "foxy" and "kooky." In this game, each of these crazy consonants takes a turn starring in two different words or names in a sentence. You get to see where the crazy consonant appears (sometimes more than once in the same word) and how many letters come before and after it. The trick is to find both words or names with the crazy consonant so that the sentence makes sense.

LOVE THAT X

1. If you ___ ___ ___ ___x your grip on the __ x, it may go flying out of your hand.

2. A ___ ___ x ___ ___ ___ ___ has ___ ___ x sides.

3. The weight lifter thought he could lift a little ___ x ___ ___ ___ weight, if he would ___ ___ ___ x his muscles before lifting.

4. The technician was trying to ___ ___ x the x-___ ___ ___ machine.

5. If you ___ ___ x shoe polish with floor ___ ___ x, you'll have a messy floor.

6. Dad says he pays enough income ___ ___ x to buy all the gold in Fort ___ ___ ___ x.

7. There's a new ___ ___ x of Wheat ___ ___ ___ x in the pantry.

8. The Rio Grande goes through both ___ ___ x ___ ___ and New ___ ___ x ___ ___ ___.

9. Richard ___ ___ x ___ ___ was first elected president in nineteen-hundred ___ ___ x ___ ___ -eight.

10. If Tinker Bell lived in Alabama, some people might have called her a ___ ___ x ___ ___ from ___ ___ x ___ ___.

ANSWER KEY

CRAZY CONSONANTS: X, J & K Love That X

1. relax, ax
2. hexagon, six
3. extra, flex
4. fix, x-ray
5. mix, wax
6. tax, Knox
7. box, Chex
8. Texas, Mexico
9. Nixon, sixty
10. pixie, Dixie

CATEGORY SCRAMBLER

HOW TO PLAY: In this game, you will be given five scrambled words. All but one of the scrambled words fits in a specific category. Unscramble the words to find the pretender. You will be given the pretender category as a clue.

FLOWERS
PRETENDER CATEGORY: SCHOOL SUPPLY

Scrambled	Unscrambled
ADIFDLOF	
TEVLOI	
LIGAMROD	
IYDSA	
NCLIPE	

ANSWER KEY

CATEGORY SCRAMBLER

Flowers: daffodil, violet, marigold, daisy

Pretender: *pencil*

PREFIX FINDER

HOW TO PLAY: An English word can consist of three parts: the root, a prefix, and a suffix. The root is the part of the word that contains its core meaning. Prefixes are attached to the beginning of a root word, and suffixes are attached to the end of the root word. Prefixes and suffixes change the word's meaning, as well as its use.

In this exercise, you will be presented with a list of words, all of which have a prefix. Your first task is to separate the root word from its prefix by drawing a line between them. Your second task is to fill in the spaces in the left-hand column with letters that correspond to the definitions in the right-hand column.

Here is an example: The word "react" can be divided into its prefix "re" and its root word "act" (re/act). Which of the following definitions matches the meaning of the prefix "re"? Is it again, next, or before? If you chose again, you made the right match. If you are not sure, try to think of other words with the same prefix, like "rebound." This will provide extra clues to the prefix's definition.

FIND THE PREFIX

1. transport ____
2. precede ____
3. circumference ____
4. midway ____
5. superintendent ____
6. defrost ____
7. polygamy ____
8. promote ____
9. subject ____
10. autobiography ____
11. irredeemable ____
12. descend ____
13. community ____
14. interwoven ____
15. antipathy ____

MATCH THE DEFINITION

a. around
b. forward, for
c. self
d. down, away
e. under
f. across
g. over, above
h. together
i. against
j. before
k. middle
l. many
m. between
n. not
o. undo, opposite

ANSWER KEY

PREFIX FINDER

1. f
2. j
3. a
4. k
5. g
6. o
7. l
8. b
9. e
10. c
11. n
12. d
13. h
14. m
15. i

SYNONYM PRETENDERS

HOW TO PLAY: Synonyms are words or phrases that mean exactly or nearly the same as another word or phrase. For example, the word "continual" is a synonym for the word "recurring," as both words mean "repeated periodically." But the word "again," which means "once more," would not be a synonym for "continual." In this next game, you must find the word that is *not* a synonym of the others.

1. Obscure
a. confuse
b. eliminate
c. befuddle
d. hide

2. Emphemeral
a. momentary
b. fleeting
c. perishable
d. brief

3. Remarkable
a. curious
b. unique
c. expensive
d. noteworthy

4. Disgusting
a. foul
b. repellent
c. antagonistic
d. loathsome

ANSWER KEY

SYNONYM PRETENDER

1. eliminate
2. perishable
3. expensive
4. antagonistic

PALINDROMES

HOW TO PLAY: A "palindrome" is a word, phrase, verse, or sentence that reads the same backward or forward. The word *dad* is an example of a simple, three-letter palindrome. In this game, you will be given a sentence with a missing word. The missing word is a palindrome. You will also be given a clue. The clue tells you the number of letters in the palindrome. Your challenge is to find the palindrome that will complete the sentence so it makes sense.

1. Clue: 5 letters

   It is your _____ duty to vote.

2. Clue: 5 letters

   The boat was equipped with _____, which helped us determine direction and depth.

3. Clue: 6 letters

   As she became more embarrassed, the color of her face got _____.

4. Clue: 3 letters

   The anchored boat started to _____ on the water when the waves picked up.

5. Clue: 5 letters

   The teacher always told us to _____ to the dictionary if we weren't sure how to spell a word.

ANSWER KEY

PALINDROMES

1. civic
2. radar
3. redder
4. bob
5. refer

HOW TO PLAY: We read English words left to right. We know where the first letter is and in which direction the letters flow to form a word. Circular words pose a greater brain challenge because the first letter can be anywhere in the circle, and the word might be read clockwise or counterclockwise.

GIRLS' NAMES

```
        N                           F
  O           I             I             R
  R           C             N             E
  E           A             I             D
        V                           W


        R                           L
  O           R             Y             T
  L           A             N             I
  E           I             N             A
        N                           K
```

ANSWER KEY

CIRCULAR WORDS Girls' Names

1. Veronica
2. Winifred
3. Lorraine
4. Kaitlynn

DITLOID PUZZLES

HOW TO PLAY: A *ditloid* is a type of word puzzle in which a phrase, quotation, or fact must be deduced from the numbers and abbreviated letters in the clue. Common words such as 'the,' 'in,' 'a,' 'an,' 'of,' etc., are usually not abbreviated. Here is an example:

12 S of the Z = 12 signs of the Zodiac

In this logic challenge, you must use the numbers and letters as clues to decipher the common phrase or place(s). A clue is given for each Ditloid. First try to solve the Ditloids with the clues in the right column covered up with your hand or a piece of paper. If you get stuck, take a peek at the clue.

Ditloid	Clue
1. 101 D	Disney movie
2. 3 B M	nursery rhyme
3. The 10 C	biblical movie
4. 20,000 L U the S	Can you swim?
5. A B and the 40 T	Arabian tale

ANSWER KEY

DITLOID PUZZLES

1. *101 Dalmatians*
2. "Three Blind Mice"
3. *The Ten Commandments*
4. *20,000 Leagues Under the Sea*
5. "Ali Baba and the 40 Thieves"

BEHEADMENTS

HOW TO PLAY: *Beheadment* sounds like something horrible and gory, but it isn't. It's a form of word play. A beheadment is a word that produces another word when you chop off the first letter. Can you figure out the missing words in the beheadment below?

I saw a man _____ an old _____ into a jewelry store.

If you came up with *bring* and its beheadment, *ring*, you'd be right. Beheadments don't always rhyme, and sometimes one word is capitalized and the other is not, but the original word and its beheaded version will always fit into a sensible sentence. Some of the sentences will have multiple beheadments, where the first letter is chopped off more than once. Your brain challenge is to fill in each sentence with the original word followed by its beheadment(s). Now off with their heads!

NATURAL KINGDOM

1. You never know exactly _____ the _____ will lay its next egg.

2. His horse almost tripped on a _____ when he went riding on a dude _____.

3. It was so quiet; you could _____ a sheep and _____ the pieces of wool fall from behind its _____.

4. A _____ is an insect and an _____ is a snake.

5. A _____ mouse can be trained to pull a _____ and get a food pellet.

ANSWER KEY

BEHEADMENTS Natural Kingdom

1. when, hen

2. branch, ranch

3. shear, hear, ear

4. wasp, asp

5. clever, lever

CURTAILMENTS

HOW TO PLAY: *Curtailments* are like beheadments, except you chop away the last letter instead of the first one. Both beheadments and curtailments change words into *new* words with *new* meanings. Can you figure out the missing words in the curtailment below?

If the old man uses his _____, he _____ walk.

If you came up with *cane* and *can*, you'd be right. As with beheadments, the idea of the game is to place the original word and its curtailed version into a sentence. The original (longer) word is the first missing word in the sentence. Some sentences have multiple curtailments, where the last letter is chopped off more than once. However, it must always be a last letter and not one that comes before. (For instance, *bow* is not a curtailment of *blown*.) Now off with their tails!

OUT & ABOUT

1. Most of the time, a _____ is _____ from the nearest big city.

2. If the rain doesn't _____ off, you may use your cassette-_____ player, but please _____ me on the shoulder if I fall asleep.

3. At the miniature-golf _____, _____ of our group made _____.

4. If I ever travel around the _____ in a _____, I'll _____ to bring something to read.

5. _____ year, I wonder if I will _____ go to Times Square on New Year's _____.

6. I spent a weekend in _____ Springs with a good _____ and his _____.

7. The _____ thought that a Cinco de _____ fiesta _____ be a good idea.

ANSWER KEY

CURTAILMENTS Out & About

1. farm, far
2. taper, tape, tap
3. party, part, par
4. planet, plane, plan
5. Every, ever, Eve
6. Palm, pal, pa
7. mayor, Mayo, may

WORD STRETCH

HOW TO PLAY: The idea in this game is to find a letter that can be put in front of each of the four given words, so that four new words can be formed with the same starting letter. For example, suppose that the four given words are: LIMB, HAIR, RASH, ORAL. If you put a "C" in front of each, you would get these four new words: CLIMB, CHAIR, CRASH, CORAL. In this exercise, find the common letter that can precede each given word set to form a whole new set of words.

Old Words	New Words
1. LANE, INCH, EACH, ROVE	P—
2. RAFT, READ, RIVER, EARTH	
3. RAIL, LASH, ETCH, LAME	
4. ROTE, OMEN, HACK, ITCH	
5. TORE, HARE, PORE, CARE	
6. AIL, ARM, EAR, ATE	
7. OFTEN, AILS, ADDLE, AGES	
8. WINE, ABLE, RACK, HERE	
9. WING, TART, LATE, WISH	
10. LEAN, OATS, ROCK, EASE	

ANSWER KEY

WORD STRETCH*

1. plane, pinch, peach, prove
2. draft, dread, driver, dearth
3. frail, flash, fetch, flame
4. wrote, women, whack, witch
5. store, share, spore, scare
6. fail, farm, fear, fate
7. soften, sails, saddle, sages
8. twine, table, track, there
9. swing, start, slate, swish
10. clean, coats, crock, cease

*There may be alternative answers not shown in this answer key.

EMBEDDED WORDS

HOW TO PLAY: Many words share letters in common. Sometimes these shared letters form another word . . . a word within a word. For example, the words *scared* and *carpet* each share the letters *c*, *a*, *r*, and *e*, which form the embedded word *care*. In this game, you will be presented with a series of embedded words broken out by theme. Your goal is to use the clue (in italics) to solve each word.

Example: __ C A R E __: *frightened*

Please note: To increase flexibility, the answers that contain the embedded words do not relate at all to each set's theme!

COFFEE

A. Your embedded word is CUP:
   1. C __ UP __: *two-door car*
   2. C __ __ __ UP: *a Heinz product*
   3. C __ U __ P __ __: *to wrinkle*
   4. C U __ P __ __ __ __: *deserving blame*
   5. __ C U __ P __ __ __ __: *an art form*

B. Your embedded word is SIP:
   1. S I __ P __ __: *very easy*
   2. S __ __ I __ P: *a shellfish*
   3. S __ I P __ __ __: *a sum of money*
   4. __ __ __ S __ I P: *a European herb*
   5. S __ I __ __ __ P: *a horse rider's foot support*

C. Your embedded word is LID:
   1. __ L __ I D: *of a Scottish pattern*
   2. L I __ __ __ D: *noted as an item*
   3. L I __ __ __ __ __ D: *an oil used in paint*
   4. __ __ __ L __ I __ __ D: *took advantage of*
   5. __ __ L I __ __ __ __ D: *infinite*

ANSWER KEY

EMBEDDED WORDS Coffee

A.

1. coupe

2. catsup

3. crumple

4. culpable

5. sculpture

B.

1. simple

2. shrimp

3. stipend

4. parsnip

5. stirrup

C.

1. plaid

2. listed

3. linseed

4. exploited

5. unlimited

WORD KNITTING

HOW TO PLAY: In this game, you are challenged to combine 20 divided words into 20 whole words by matching the front and back halves of each word together. The words are not necessarily divided by syllable. For example, when you match "TRIU" with "MPH," they combine to make TRIUMPH. Cross off your matches as you go along.

COMMON & EXOTIC PETS

OG	GER	CHI	TUR	HOG
KEET	RAB	MON	PARA	CRAB
FER	TLE	SN	CHIN	TARAN
HERMIT	HAM	LI	MA	WALLA
SE	HEDGE	KEY	BIL	AKE
PIR	BY	THON	RET	PY
ZARD	TULA	ANHA	CHILLA	CAW
STER	HOR	FR	HUAHUA	BIT

ANSWER KEY

WORD KNITTING Common & Exotic Pets

Chihuahua
chinchilla
ferret
frog
gerbil
hamster
hedgehog
hermit crab
horse
lizard
macaw
monkey
parakeet
piranha
python
rabbit
snake
tarantula
turtle
wallaby

WORD MULTIPLIER

HOW TO PLAY: You will be presented with a grid containing letters that make up a common word. Your challenge is to mix and match the letters to make as many new words as possible. Each new word should contain four or more letters. Vowels can be used more than once in the same new word. You will be playing against a computer program that generated new words, based on the letters in each grid. How many new words can you come up with? See if you can match or beat the computer!

LATER GATOR

When presented with this challenge, the computer found 11 words with four letters or more.

L		A
	T	
E		R

NEW WORDS:

ANSWER KEY

WORD MULTIPLIER Later Gator

alert, alter, earl, late, leer, rate, real, reel, tale, teal, tear

QUADRUPLETS

HOW TO PLAY: Your brain challenge is to discover the word that can be added to a quadruplet set of words to form new words or phrases. The word they have in common may go before or after the presented word. The puzzle title is your clue to the word that can be glued to all four words. Or start with the set and work your way back to solving the puzzle title. When you decode the puzzle title, you will have the "common" word that completes the set.

Look at the example in the box below.

> ## TITLE: AN AMERICAN PASTIME
> 1. black
> 2. park
> 3. point
> 4. fire

What compound word does the title refer to? That's right, baseball. Now which half of this compound word can be linked to the four words in the set to create four new compound words? If you guessed ball, you're right again. Put it to the test: add ball to each of the words below (as a prefix or suffix) and see what you get. You've succeeded if your four new words are: *blackball*, *ballpark*, *ballpoint*, and *fireball*.

FORMER CATERPILLAR

1. dragon
2. fire
3. bar
4. swatter

ICY FIGURE

1. shoe
2. storm
3. board
4. flake

BOATER'S SOS

1. birth
2. light
3. dream
4. dooms

ANSWER KEY

QUADRUPLETS

Former Caterpillar
fly—butterfly

Icy Figure
snow—snowman

Boater's SOS
day—Mayday

BEHEADMENTS

HOW TO PLAY: *Beheadment* sounds like something horrible and gory, but it isn't. It's a form of word play. A beheadment is a word that produces another word when you chop off the first letter. Can you figure out the missing words in the beheadment below?

I saw a man _____ an old _____ into a jewelry store.

If you came up with *bring* and its beheadment, *ring*, you'd be right. Beheadments don't always rhyme, and sometimes one word is capitalized and the other is not, but the original word and its beheaded version will always fit into a sensible sentence. Some of the sentences will have multiple beheadments, where the first letter is chopped off more than once. Your brain challenge is to fill in each sentence with the original word followed by its beheadment(s). Now off with their heads!

OUTDOORS

1. The river may _____ up if another _____ falls into it.

2. It's not supposed to _____ anymore _____ that spring is here.

3. A drunk _____ drove right into the _____.

4. People go to the beach to play in the _____ _____ the water.

5. The farmer had to _____ the field even though the temperature was uncomfortably _____.

ANSWER KEY

BEHEADMENTS Outdoors

1. clog, log
2. snow, now
3. driver, river
4. sand, and
5. plow, low

HOMONYM PAIRS

HOW TO PLAY: In this game, you will use clues to determine pairs of *homonyms*, words that have the same sound but are spelled differently and have different meanings.

Clues	Homonym Pairs
out-of-work movie star	*idle, idol*
forest female with money	*doe, dough*

Clues	Homonym Pairs
a. a dull A+	
b. Helsinki stopping point	
c. Warsaw vote	
d. count them: sight, smell, taste, touch, hearing	
e. a hurled seat of power	
f. 3.14159 dessert	
g. a narrow sea passage without curves	
h. a proud barn topper	

ANSWER KEY

HOMONYM PAIRS

a. grayed, grade

b. Finnish, finish

c. Pole, poll

d. census, senses

e. thrown, throne

f. pi, pie

g. strait, straight

h. vain, vane

HINKY PINKY

HOW TO PLAY: Hinky Pinky is a word game that consists of two clues for which the answer is two words that rhyme. In this game, you will be given clues and asked to determine pairs of single-syllable rhymes. Here are three examples:

red sled = rouge luge

penniless Brit = broke bloke

dog's face = pug mug

1. a quick present

2. a toy that flies, in a battle

3. floor squares within a linear walkway

4. a pond-hopper's street

5. a little athletic competition

6. an algebra or trig route

7. a certain remedy

8. kingly black gold

9. a frothy, bubbly residence

10. a toothed-wheel phobia

ANSWER KEY

HINKY PINKY

1. swift gift
2. kite fight
3. tile aisle
4. toad road
5. short sport
6. math path
7. sure cure
8. royal oil
9. foam home
10. gear fear

HIDDEN WORDS

HOW TO PLAY: In this game, you will be presented with a series of sentences. Each sentence contains a hidden word made up of sequential letters. Your challenge is to find the hidden word. The "set title" provides a clue to the hidden words.

Example: A PERSON IN A <u>RUT HA</u>S TO GET OUT OF IT.

BIBLICAL NAMES

1. A LAWYER MUST FORMAT THE WILL CORRECTLY.

2. SOME PEOPLE READ AVIDLY.

3. MOST EXPERTS RATE VASSAR AHEAD OF BENNINGTON.

4. THE PEOPLE OF TAMPA ULTIMATELY GOT A BASEBALL TEAM.

5. DON'T PUT THE PIANO AHEAD OF YOUR ACADEMIC COURSES.

HIDDEN WORDS Biblical Names

1. Matthew
2. David
3. Sarah
4. Paul
5. Noah

1. A LAWYER MUST FOR<u>MAT THE W</u>ILL CORRECTLY.

2. SOME PEOPLE REA<u>D AVID</u>LY.

3. MOST EXPERTS RATE VAS<u>SAR AH</u>EAD OF BENNINGTON.

4. THE PEOPLE OF TAM<u>PA UL</u>TIMATELY GOT A BASEBALL TEAM.

5. DON'T PUT THE PIA<u>NO AH</u>EAD OF YOUR ACADEMIC COURSES.

WORD LADDERS

HOW TO PLAY: Word Ladders is a game invented by Lewis Carroll. In this brain challenge, you will be given a *start word* and an *end word*. To solve the puzzle, you must change the start word into the end word progressively. Each progressive step generates a new word, which consists of a single letter substitution. Below is an example of a word ladder that goes from "cold" to "warm."

cold → cord → card → ward → warm

MAN TO NUT

man
nut

FIND TO LOSE

find
lose

ANSWER KEY

WORD LADDERS*

Man to Nut

man, mat, met, net, nut

Find to Lose

find, fine, line, lone, lose

*There may be alternative answers not shown in this answer key.

LETTER ZAP

HOW TO PLAY: The idea in this game is to find the name of a popular television series by zapping a given number of letters from a nonsense phrase and reading the remaining letters in order. For example, if you zap the 5 letters *y, B, y, M,* and *i* from the phrase *Wily Bland Gray Mice,* you'll be left with the television series *Will and Grace.* The answer for each letter-zap clue below is a show that is or was highly popular and long running.

1. *Fried Hands* — zap 3 (NYC sitcom)

2. *Play Wand Border* — zap 3 (legal drama)

3. *Sure Evil Vower* — zap 5 (reality adventure)

4. *These Limp Stones* — zap 4 (cartoon sitcom)

5. *Jet Top Hardly!* — zap 4 (heady game show)

ANSWER KEY

LETTER ZAP

1. *Friends*
2. *Law and Order*
3. *Survivor*
4. *The Simpsons*
5. *Jeopardy!*

SOMETHING IN COMMON

How to Play: "Something in Common" puzzles have five items in one column (Column A) and five items in another column (Column B). The goal is to find what all the things in Column A have in common, which none of the things in Column B have in common. To solve the puzzle, start with Column A, and find a common denominator among the items. Examples of common denominators are physical locations, arrangement of consonants and vowels, parts of speech, numeric relationships, etc. Once you believe that you have found the common denominator, cross-check against the items in Column B. None of the items in Column B should share this common denominator.

1.
COLUMN A	**COLUMN B**
cope	piglet
kept	tall
graph	flag
type	open
happy	ship

2.
COLUMN A	**COLUMN B**
Rhode Island	Maine
New York	Kentucky
North Carolina	Oregon
South Dakota	Georgia
West Virginia	Illinois

ANSWER KEY

SOMETHING IN COMMON

1. the second-to-the-last letter is "p"

2. two-word states

TRIPLETS

How to Play: Your brain challenge is to discover the word that can be added to each of three words to form three new words or phrases. The word they have in common may go before or after the presented word. The puzzle title is your clue to the word that can be glued to all three words. Or start with the trio set and work your way back to solving the puzzle title. When you decode the puzzle title, you will have the "common" word that completes the set. Look at the example in the box below.

> ## TITLE: DELAY TACTIC
> 1. faced
> 2. brown
> 3. stepping

What compound word can make up the title? If you guessed *stonewall*, you're right. Now, which one of these two words can be linked to the three words in the set to create three new compound words? Exactly, *stone*. So the three new words are: *stone-faced*, *brownstone*, and *stepping stone*.

TITLE 1: TICKET SALES
1. boom
2. car
3. sand

TITLE 2: FITNESS ROUTINE
1. net
2. shop
3. busy

TITLE 3: CIRCUS EMCEE
1. brass
2. worm
3. wedding

ANSWER KEY

TRIPLETS

1. box — box office

2. work — workout

3. ring — ringmaster

CHARADES

How to Play: Charades might have started as a word game, not the acting game that is more familiar today. For this version of charades, first solve the clues by coming up with a new word that is equal in meaning to each original clue word. Then combine the two new words to create a solution that explains the puzzle's title.

Puzzle Example:

Title: Full of Vinegar

Clues:
a. whiz = *ace*
b. twitch = *tic*

Solution: *ace+tic = acetic* = **Title:** Full of Vinegar [acetic is a property of vinegar]

Title 1: Gondola's Place
  a. soup container
  b. Gore's name

Title 2: Woody Plant
  a. loud thud
  b. ghostly greeting

Title 3: Sell Out
  a. wager
  b. bit of sunshine

ANSWER KEY

CHARADES

1. can+al = canal
2. bam+boo = bamboo
3. bet+ray = betray

SUFFIX MATCH

HOW TO PLAY: An English word can consist of three parts: the *root*, a *prefix*, and a *suffix*. The root is the part of the word that contains its core meaning. Prefixes are attached to the beginning of a root word, and suffixes are attached to the end of the root word. Prefixes and suffixes change the word's meaning as well as its use.

In this exercise, you will be presented with a list of words, all of which have a suffix. Your first task is to separate the root word from its suffix by drawing a line between them. Your second task is to fill in the space following the word with the letter that corresponds to the correct definition of the suffix.

Here is an example: The word *biblical* ends with the suffix "*ical*," which is common in many words, including those that are historical, medical, and musical. Which of the following definitions matches the meaning of the suffix "*ical*"?

a. full of
b. having to do with
c. resembling

If you chose "*having to do with*," you made the correct suffix match.

FIND THE SUFFIX

1. communism __
2. hopeless __
3. claustrophobia __
4. adventurous __
5. appendectomy __
6. biology __
7. physician __
8. asteroid __
9. herbicide __
10. fellowship __

MATCH THE DEFINITION

a. study, field of
b. cutting, part removal
c. resembling, shaped like
d. one who has skill, art
e. a position or state of being
f. kill, killing
g. without
h. exaggerated fear
i. full of
j. belief in

ANSWER KEY

SUFFIX MATCH

1. j
2. g
3. h
4. i
5. b
6. a
7. d
8. c
9. f
10. e

WORD PYRAMIDS

HOW TO PLAY: In a word-pyramid game, you will create a new word each time you move down the pyramid levels. This is done by adding a letter to the previous word, and therefore increasing the word size by one letter. The new word will contain the previous word; however, the letters will usually need to be rearranged to form the new word. For each level of the pyramid, you are given two clues to help you create the new word:

a description of the new word and the new letter to be added to form the new word.

Japanese wine

Hockey equipment (+T)

Red Riding Hood's prop (+B)

A hurdle to overcome (+C)

ANSWER KEY

WORD PYRAMIDS

sake, skate, basket, setback

HOMONYM PAIRS

HOW TO PLAY: In this game, you will use clues to determine pairs of *homonyms,* words that have the same sound but are spelled differently and have different meanings.

Clues
out-of-work movie star
forest female with money

Homonym Pairs
idle, idol
doe, dough

Clues	Homonym Pairs
a. fixed writing materials	
b. a T-bone peg	
c. a boat-pier healer	
d. peacock's proud story	
e. a will-beneficiary mistake	
f. Olympics: took a single medal	
g. an acting part for a dinner bread	
h. consumed a black billiard ball	

ANSWER KEY

HOMONYM PAIRS

a. stationary, stationery

b. steak, stake

c. dock, doc

d. tail, tale

e. heir, err

f. won, one

g. role, roll

h. ate, eight

SOMETHING IN COMMON

HOW TO PLAY: "Something in Common" puzzles have five items in one column (Column A) and five items in another column (Column B). The goal is to find what all the things in Column A have in common, which none of the things in Column B have in common. To solve the puzzle, start with Column A, and find a common denominator among the items. Examples of common denominators are physical locations, arrangement of consonant and vowels, parts of speech, numeric relationships, etc. Once you believe that you have found the common denominator, cross-check against the items in Column B. None of the items in Column B should share this common denominator.

1.

COLUMN A	COLUMN B
Jose	Isaac
Renee	Alice
Denise	Gina
Abdul	Heather
Louise	Patrick

2.

COLUMN A	COLUMN B
electrical cord	washing machine
toaster	bathtub
paint thinner	dresser
candle	closet
cigarette	sink

ANSWER KEY

SOMETHING IN COMMON

1. names with an accent on the second syllable

2. things that can cause fires

RIGHT BRAIN

CAN YOU SEE IT?

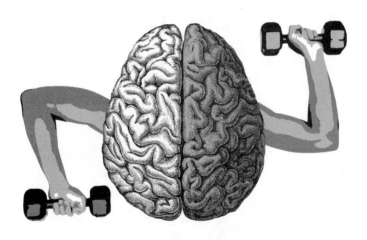

RIGHT BRAIN: CAN YOU SEE IT?
VISUAL PERCEPTION & SPATIAL EXERCISES

INTRODUCTION:
The focus of the exercises in this section will be on the right brain's visual-spatial processing strengths. In this workout, your brain will light up as it "sees" the possibilities in the patterns. The puzzles relate to:

LEFT   RIGHT

Creativity

Imagination

Holistic Thinking

Intuition

Arts

Daydreaming

Nonverbal Communication

Visualization

Feelings

Tunes of Songs

Rhythm

ODD ONE OUT

HOW TO PLAY: In this puzzle you will see a group of images. Try to find the image that is different from the rest. In the example below, can you guess which letter is the odd one out?

C B Q W D

All the letters in the example have curved lines, except for only one letter, which has straight lines. "W" is the odd one out.

SHIFTING SHAPES
Which shape has different properties from the rest?

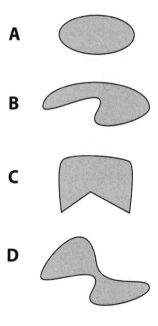

A

B

C

D

ANSWER KEY

ODD ONE OUT Shifting Shapes

Shape C is the odd one out because it is the only shape with sharp lines.

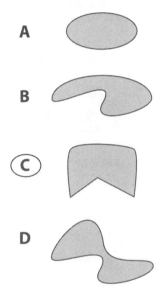

NEXT IN LINE

HOW TO PLAY: In this exercise, your right-brain challenge is to identify the figure that would logically complete the sequence. The key to the sequence is in the visual pattern. In each sequence, there is a "rule" that orders the pattern. Choose from shapes A, B, C, or D below for the answer. Use the logic questions in each exercise to guide you to the correct selection.

SHAPE SHIFTING

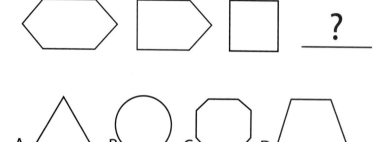

LOGIC STEPS:

1. Consider the question you have to answer: What is the next shape in the sequence?

2. What do you know already? The shapes are different. How? They all have a different number of sides.

3. What is the pattern? The shapes have a smaller number of sides as they progress.

4. What is the answer? Now, trace the pattern in your own mind. What might be the next step in this pattern? Make your best guess before you look at the possible answers. You might be surprised that you can pick it out easily.

ANSWER KEY

NEXT IN LINE

Set One: Shape Shifting

A. The answer is shape A because the shapes on the first line are diminishing by one side at a time.

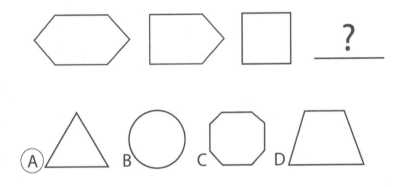

MAZE HAZE

HOW TO PLAY: Use your right brain to see your way through the following maze. Trace an unobstructed path, beginning at the "Start" and ending at the "Finish."

SINK OR SWIM

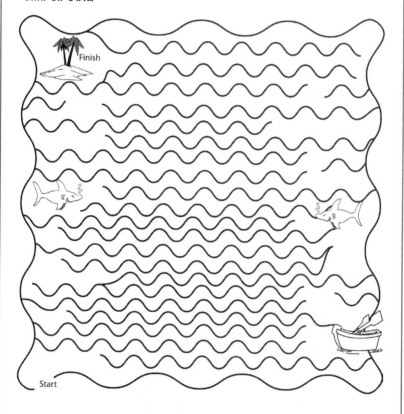

MAZE HAZE Sink or Swim

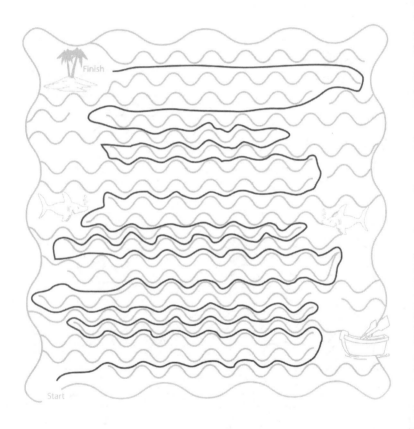

COMPARE AND CONTRAST

HOW TO PLAY: In this exercise, you will see two pictures side by side that appear to be exact replicas. But they are not. Your challenge is to identify how the second picture is different from the first. It may have things missing, or things added to it.

CLOWNING AROUND

Find the five differences between the two images.

ANSWER KEY

COMPARE AND CONTRAST Clowning Around

1. missing polka dots on clown hat

2. missing expression lines over clown's eyes

3. missing white accent on nose

4. missing polka dots on tie collar

5. missing white creases in the center of big tie

ENTANGLEMENTS

HOW TO PLAY: In this brain teaser, you will see a layered image. Your challenge is to identify and circle the *three* singular images that must be combined to create the layered image at the top.

FALLING LEAVES

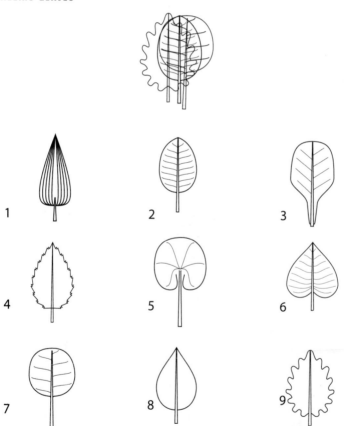

1

2

3

4

5

6

7

8

9

ANSWER KEY

ENTANGLEMENTS Falling Leaves

Images 2, 7, and 9 create the layered image at the top.

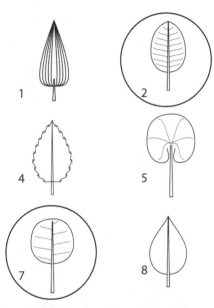

RECONSTRUCTION

HOW TO PLAY: In this brain challenge, you must identify the set of shapes that make up the whole image.

BROKEN CIRCLE
Which set of broken shapes makes up the whole circle?

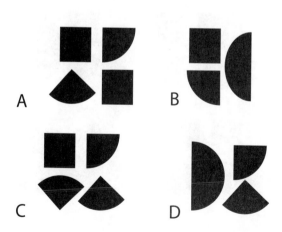

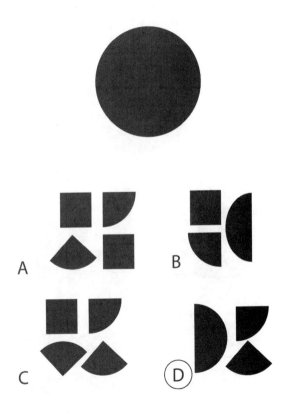

TWISTS & TURNS

HOW TO PLAY: In this exercise, your right-brain challenge is to identify the correct match in response to the question posed. To do so, your right brain will need to be in high gear as you twist, turn, rotate, and flip images in your mind to find the right match. Individuals who have a strong right-brain orientation will be able to see the correct match. For the rest of us, the guiding questions will help us by tapping into our left-brain logic.

FLOORED

Which one of the four plans below *matches* the original floor plan above?

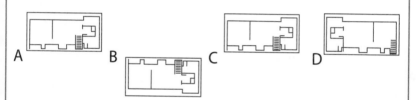

A B C D

LOGIC STEPS:

1. Consider your goal: to find which floor plan (A, B, C, or D) matches the floor plan at the top.

2. What do you know already? The four floor plans look different. But one of them matches the top one. We need to look for similarities. It might be that a floor plan is rotated and presents a seemingly different view.

3. What is the pattern? Start to look for similar walls. Look for similar placement of the doors. Are the stair steps in the same location and orientation?

4. What is the answer? If you are stuck, trace the original floor plan and move it over the others.

ANSWER KEY

TWISTS & TURNS Floored

C. If you mentally rotate the floor plan C 180 degrees, you will see that it matches the floor plan at the top.

OPTICAL ILLUSIONS

HOW TO PLAY: Optical illusions play tricks with the way your brain receives visual stimuli. Answering the question below is a key to solving the illusion of the "leggy elephant."

LEGGY ELEPHANT
How many legs does the elephant have?

ANSWER KEY

OPTICAL ILLUSIONS Leggy Elephant

The elephant has eight "legs," if you count the images in the foreground (with hooves) and the images in the background (without hooves).

MOSAICS

HOW TO PLAY: In this exercise, you will be presented with four images. All but one of the images appear in the mosaic picture that follows. Your brain challenge is to identify the image that is not part of the collage.

BIRDIE

1

2

3

4

ANSWER KEY

MOSAICS Birdie

Image 1 is not part of the collage.

1   2   3   4

COMPARE AND CONTRAST

HOW TO PLAY: In this exercise, you will see two pictures side by side that appear to be exact replicas. But they are not. Your challenge is to identify how the second picture is different from the first. It may have things missing, or things added to it.

SAILING

Find the five differences between the two images.

ANSWER KEY

COMPARE AND CONTRAST Sailing

1. mast tower cages have different number of lines and spaces
2. mast tower cage is suspended by one solid line rather than three
3. medium-size white sail is missing a cross symbol
4. small white sail is missing
5. left side of boat is missing a white window

ODD ONE OUT

How to Play: In this puzzle, you will see a group of images. Try to find the image that is different from the rest. In the example below, can you guess which letter is the odd one out?

C B Q W D

All the letters in the example have curved lines, except for only one letter, which has straight lines. "W" is the odd one out.

Umbrella Girl
Which girl doesn't have a twin?

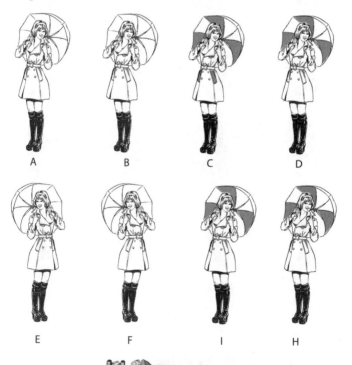

ANSWER KEY

ODD ONE OUT Umbrella Girl

Umbrella Girl C is the odd one out because she's the only girl with shaded coat pockets.

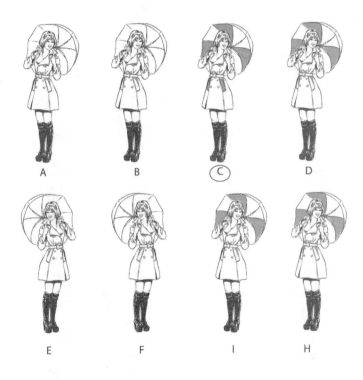

A   B   C   D

E   F   I   H

OPTICAL ILLUSIONS

HOW TO PLAY: Optical illusions play tricks with the way your brain receives visual stimuli. For the illusion, a question will be posed. Answering the question below is a key to solving the illusion.

SIZE IT UP
Which figure has the larger circle in the middle of it?

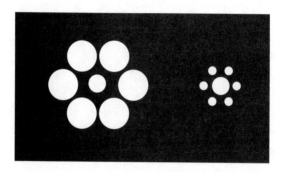

SOLVING THE ILLUSION:

1. Consider the challenge you have to solve: There are two figures above. Each one has a center circle. You are to determine which of the two center circles is the larger circle.

2. What do you know already? Each center circle is surrounded by six larger or smaller circles. One of the center circles seems larger than the other. You must select the one that truly is larger.

3. What is the pattern? One figure has six outside circles that are much bigger than the outside circles of the other figure. They may be in the illusion to distract us. Ask yourself why they are in the illusion at all.

4. Concentrate your vision on the two center circles. Ignore the outside circles. Which figure has the larger circle in the middle of it?

ANSWER KEY

OPTICAL ILLUSIONS Size It Up

Neither one of the inner circles is larger than the other. Cover the outer circles and you will see that the two inner circles are the same size.

NEXT IN LINE

HOW TO PLAY: In this exercise, your right-brain challenge is to identify the figure that would logically complete the sequence. The key to the sequence is in the visual pattern. In each sequence, there is a "rule" that orders the pattern. Choose from shapes A, B, C, or D below for the answer. Use the logic questions in each exercise to guide you to the correct selection.

MOVING STARS

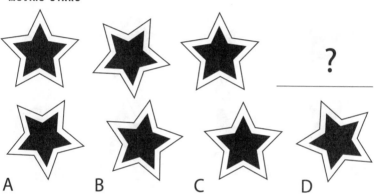

A   B   C   D

LOGIC QUESTIONS:

1. Consider the question you have to answer: What is the next figure in the sequence?

2. What do you already know about the figures?

3. What do they have in common?

4. What is the relationship among the figures?
      a. number of sides?   d. shading of figures?
      b. direction of figures?   e. movement of figures?
      c. relationship between the figures?   f. combinations of figures?

5. What is the pattern rule?

ANSWER KEY

NEXT IN LINE Moving Stars

The answer is figure A. The first and third star are the same, so the second and fourth star should match each other.

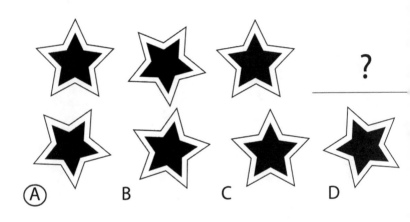

OPTICAL ILLUSIONS

How to Play: Optical illusions play tricks with the way your brain receives visual stimuli. For the illusion, a question will be posed. Answering the question below is a key to solving the illusion.

Two-Headed Critter
There are two critters in this illusion . . . one lives on land, and the other in the water. What are they?

ANSWER KEY

OPTICAL ILLUSIONS Two-Headed Critter

The two critters are a duck and a rabbit.

ENTANGLEMENTS

HOW TO PLAY: In this brain teaser, you will see a layered image. Your challenge is to identify and circle the *three* singular images that must be combined to create the layered image at the top.

AVIARY

1

2

3

4

5

6

7

8

9

ANSWER KEY

ENTANGLEMENTS Aviary

Images 2, 7, and 8 create the layered image at the top.

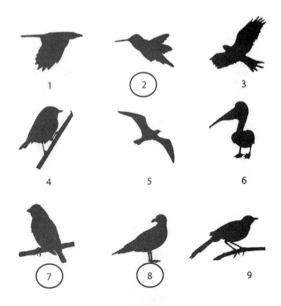

COMPARE AND CONTRAST

HOW TO PLAY: In this exercise, you will see two pictures side by side that appear to be exact replicas. But they are not. Your challenge is to identify how the second picture is different from the first.

MUSICAL THEATRE

Find the eight differences between the two images.

ANSWER KEY

COMPARE AND CONTRAST Musical Theatre

1. side accent lines on left mask are pointing to the sides instead of down
2. musical note is missing in the first upper right cluster of notes
3. top ballet slipper is missing lacing cross lines
4. not enough strings on the lowest cord grouping of the violin
5. no accent circle on top of left-side groove of the violin
6. no accent circle on bottom of left-side groove of the violin
7. no accent circle on top of right-side groove of the violin
8. no accent circle on bottom of right-side groove of the violin

MAZE HAZE

HOW TO PLAY: Use your right brain to see your way through the following maze. Trace an unobstructed path, beginning at the "Start" and ending at the "Finish."

INTERLOCKING CIRCLES

ANSWER KEY

MAZE HAZE Interlocking Circles

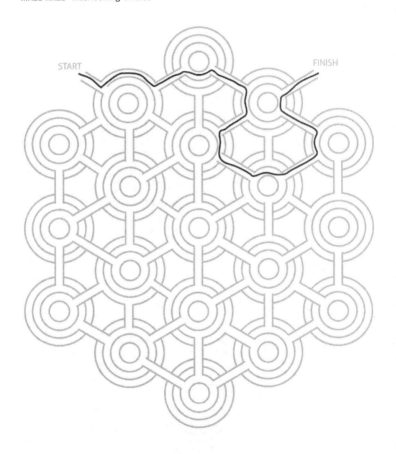

START   FINISH

NEXT IN LINE

HOW TO PLAY: In this exercise, your right-brain challenge is to identify the figure that would logically complete the sequence. The key to the sequence is in the visual pattern. In each sequence, there is a "rule" that orders the pattern. Choose from shapes A, B, C, or D below for the answer. Use the logic questions in each exercise to guide you to the correct selection.

ARROW ROTATIONS

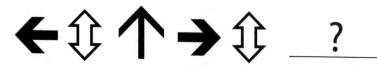

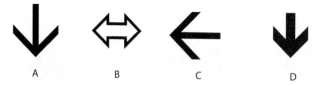

A   B   C   D

LOGIC QUESTIONS:

1. Consider the question you have to answer: What is the next figure in the sequence?

2. What do you already know about the figures?

3. What do they have in common?

4. What is the relationship among the figures?
   - a. number of sides?
   - b. direction of figures?
   - c. relationship between the figures?
   - d. shading of figures?
   - e. movement of figures?
   - f. combinations of figures?

5. What is the pattern rule?

NEXT IN LINE Arrow Rotations

The answer is figure A. The pattern is bold arrow pointing left, white arrow pointing up and down, thin arrow pointing up; then, bold arrow pointing right, white arrow pointing up and down, and thin arrow pointing down.

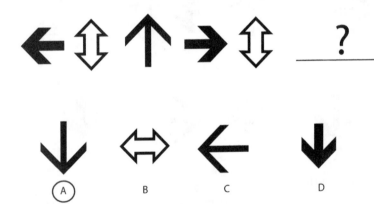

ODD ONE OUT

HOW TO PLAY: In this puzzle, you will see a group of images. Look at the images. Try to find the image that is different from the rest. Example: Look at the letters below. Which letter is the odd one out?

C B Q W D

One letter is made with straight lines, while all the others have curved lines. In this example, "W" is the odd one out.

CORNICES

Which image is the odd one out?

A

B

C

D

ANSWER KEY

ODD ONE OUT Cornices

Image C is the odd one out because the bottom curlicues are oversized.

A

B

C

D

MOSAICS

HOW TO PLAY: In this exercise, you will be presented with four images. All but one of the images appear in the mosaic picture that follows. Your brain challenge is to identify the image that is not part of the collage.

REINDEER

1

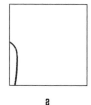
2

3

4

ANSWER KEY

MOSAICS Reindeer

Image 2 is not part of the collage.

1

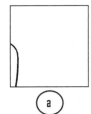

3

3

4

ENTANGLEMENTS

HOW TO PLAY: In this brain teaser, you will see a layered image. Your challenge is to identify and circle the *three* singular images that must be combined to create the layered image at the top.

WARDROBE

1

2

3

4

5

6

7

8

9

ANSWER KEY

ENTANGLEMENTS Wardrobe

Images 4, 8, and 9 create the layered image at the top.

MAZE HAZE

HOW TO PLAY: Use your right brain to see your way through the
following maze. Trace an unobstructed path, beginning at the "Start"
and ending at the "Finish."

ROARING LION

START

FINISH

ANSWER KEY

MAZE HAZE Roaring Lion

START

FINISH

OPTICAL ILLUSIONS

HOW TO PLAY: In this brain challenge, you will be presented with two optical illusions. Optical illusions play tricks with the way your brain receives visual stimuli. For each illusion, a question will be posed. Answering the question will help you see your way toward solving the illusion.

MIRROR IMAGES

The foreground and background are reversible in this illusion, creating two distinct pictures. What two images do you see?

ANSWER KEY

OPTICAL ILLUSIONS Mirror Images

The images are a vase in white and two faces in black.

COMPARE AND CONTRAST

HOW TO PLAY: In this exercise, you will see two pictures side by side that appear to be exact replicas. But they are not. Your challenge is to identify how the second picture is different from the first.

FLORAL PATTERN

Find the five differences between the two images.

ANSWER KEY

COMPARE AND CONTRAST Floral Pattern

1. center swirled stem is turned to the left instead of the right

2. black floral design on the right is missing a petal in the top outer grouping

3. black floral design on the right is missing a set of small, dropping circles at the bottom

4. middle center design has black shading

5. lower left floral grouping has only one outer leaf

ODD ONE OUT

HOW TO PLAY: In this puzzle, you will see a group of images. Look at the images. Try to find the image that is different from the rest. Example: Look at the letters below. Which letter is the odd one out?

C B Q W D

One letter is made with straight lines, while all the others have curved lines. In this example, "W" is the odd one out.

CIRCLES & SHAPES

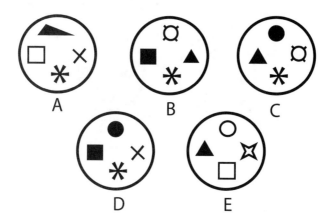

Which circle contains images that don't fit with the pattern of the others?

ANSWER KEY

ODD ONE OUT Circles & Shapes

The answer is D. This is the only image that has all the shapes inside filled in. The other images have at least one shape that is not filled in.

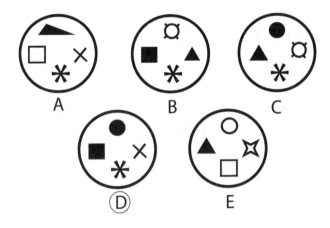

ENTANGLEMENTS

HOW TO PLAY: In this brain teaser, you will see a layered image. Your challenge is to identify the three singular images that must be combined to create the layered image at the top.

FOODIE

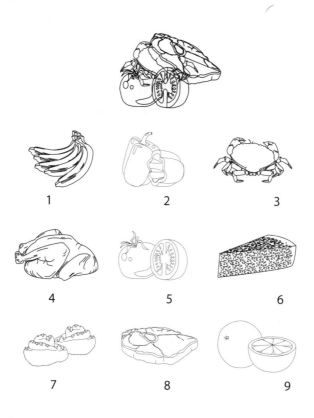

1

2

3

4

5

6

7

8

9

Answer Key

ENTANGLEMENTS Foodie

Images 3, 5, and 8 create the layered image at the top.

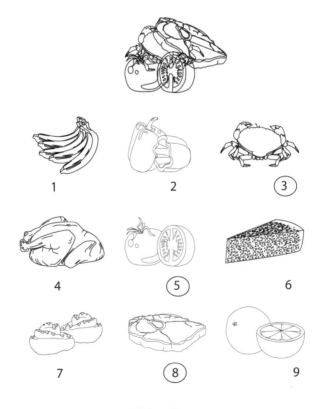

COPYCAT

HOW TO PLAY: This exercise involves both memory and visual perception. You have two grids: one has a graphic design superimposed on it, and the other one is blank. Your brain challenge is to reproduce the graphic design on the top by drawing every element of it in the same location on the blank grid on the bottom.

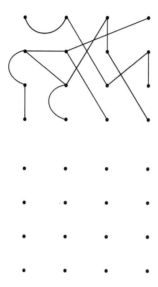

ANSWER KEY

COPYCAT

Compare your graphic grid to the original grid. How close did you come to a perfect reproduction?

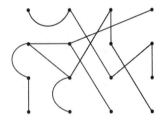

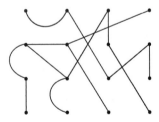

COMPARE AND CONTRAST

HOW TO PLAY: In this exercise, you will see two pictures side by side that appear to be exact replicas. But they are not. Your challenge is to identify how the second picture is different from the first. It may have things missing, or things added to it. There are five differences between the first image and the second image.

MERRY-GO-ROUND

Find the five differences between the two images.

ANSWER KEY

COMPARE AND CONTRAST Merry-Go-Round

1. The flag is filled in.

2. The second semicircular shape above the horses is filled in.

3. The third semicircular shape above the horses is missing a fifth bulb.

4. The horse in the center is filled in.

5. On the extreme left of the merry-go-round, the horse in back has changed from black to white.

 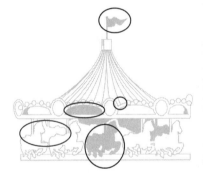

NEXT IN LINE

HOW TO PLAY: In this exercise, your right-brain challenge is to identify the figure that would logically complete the sequence. The key to the sequence is in the visual pattern. In each sequence, there is a "rule" that orders the pattern.

SQUARE IT!
Determine the next box in the sequence.

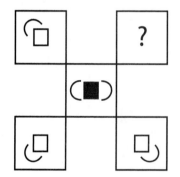

A

B

C

D

ANSWER KEY

NEXT IN LINE Square It!

The answer is B. All the squares on the outside of the figure are clear; therefore, the answer will have a clear square. The arcs move to reflect the position of the square, so the answer will have an arc in the upper right, which reflects the position of the box in the grid.

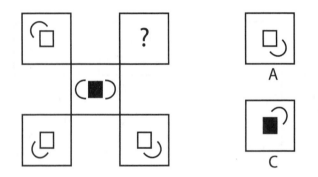

OPTICAL ILLUSIONS

HOW TO PLAY: In this brain challenge, you will be presented with two optical illusions. Optical illusions play tricks with the way your brain receives visual stimuli. For each illusion, a question will be posed. Answering the question will help you see your way toward solving the illusion.

ARROWS & CATS
How many inside and outside arrows do you see in the figure below left? How many cats do you see in the figure below right?

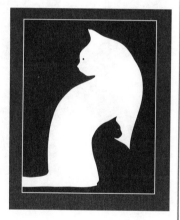

ANSWER KEY

OPTICAL ILLUSIONS Arrows & Cats

Arrows = 8 [four black and four white]

Cats = 2 [one black and one white]

NEXT IN LINE

HOW TO PLAY: In this exercise, your right-brain challenge is to identify the figure that would logically complete the sequence. The key to the sequence is in the visual pattern. In each sequence, there is a "rule" that orders the pattern. Choose from shapes A, B, C, or D below for the answer.

SPIN THE WHEEL

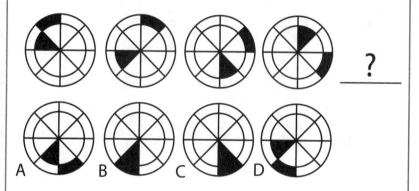

?

A   B   C   D

ANSWER KEY

NEXT IN LINE Spin the Wheel

The answer is A. The correct answer takes the movement within both rings into account. The black rectangle section in the outer ring is moving clockwise one space. The black triangle section in the inner ring is moving counterclockwise one space.

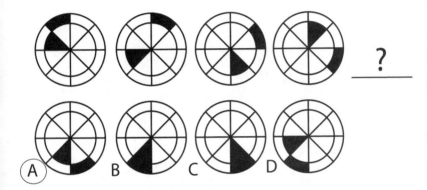

MOSAICS

How to Play: In this exercise, you will be presented with a set of four images. All but one of the images appear in the mosaic picture that follows. Your brain challenge is to identify the image that is not part of the collage.

FLORAL

1

2

3

4

MOSAICS Floral

Image 3 is not part of the mosaic.

ODD ONE OUT

HOW TO PLAY: In this puzzle, you will see a group of images. Look at the images. Try to find the image that is different from the rest. Example: Look at the letters below. Which letter is the odd one out?

C B Q W D

One letter is made with straight lines, while all the others have curved lines. In this example, "W" is the odd one out.

BOXES, DOTS & LINES

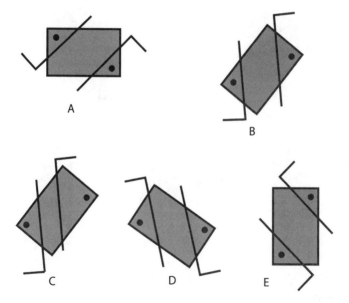

A

B

C

D

E

Which image doesn't fit the pattern?

ODD ONE OUT Boxes, Dots & Lines

The answer is C. This is the only image in which the "L" lines don't create two triangles within the rectangle.

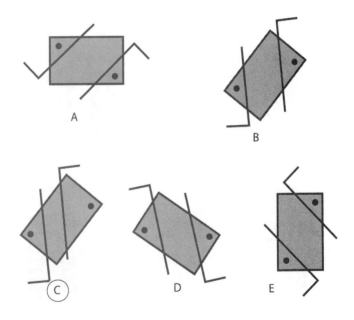

A

B

C

D

E

OPTICAL ILLUSIONS

HOW TO PLAY: Optical illusions play tricks with the way your brain receives visual stimuli. For the illusion, a question will be posed. Answering the question below is a key to solving the illusion.

YOUNG WOMAN, OLD WOMAN
Can you see the young woman and the old woman in this same drawing?

ANSWER KEY

OPTICAL ILLUSIONS Young Woman, Old Woman

Young woman: The young woman is in a full profile — see her shapely chin and long neck with a choker?

Old woman: The young woman's chin becomes the nose of the old woman; the young woman's choker becomes the mouth of the old woman; the young woman's left ear becomes the left eye of the old woman.

NEXT IN LINE

HOW TO PLAY: In this exercise, your right-brain challenge is to identify the figure that would logically complete the sequence. The key to the sequence is in the visual pattern. In each sequence, there is a "rule" that orders the pattern.

ACROBAT
Determine the next figure in the sequence

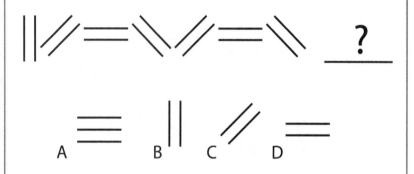

ANSWER KEY

NEXT IN LINE Twelve: Acrobat

The answer is figure B. If you take the title into account, you can see an acrobat (two parallel lines) starting in a standing position, and then tumbling into a horizontal position, and then moving up and over again, ending in a standing position. Another way to solve the puzzle is to see that the final figure is a reverse of the first.

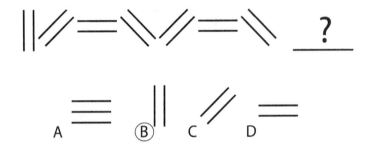

COMPARE AND CONTRAST

HOW TO PLAY: In this exercise, you will see two pictures side by side that appear to be exact replicas. But they are not. Your challenge is to identify how the second picture is different from the first. It may have things missing, or things added to it. There are five differences between the first image and the second image.

BIRD OR FISH

Find the five differences between the two images.

ANSWER KEY

COMPARE AND CONTRAST Bird or Fish

1. The first head plume (moving from left to right) is missing a feather.

2. The third head plume (moving from left to right) is missing an additional shape.

3. The middle tail plume is missing a circular shape at the top.

4. Three small feathers are missing under the middle belly.

5. An inner shape is missing on the first leg.

NEXT IN LINE

HOW TO PLAY: In this exercise, your right-brain challenge is to identify the figure that would logically complete the sequence. The key to the sequence is in the visual pattern. In each sequence, there is a "rule" that orders the pattern.

SQUARES
Determine the next figure in the sequence.

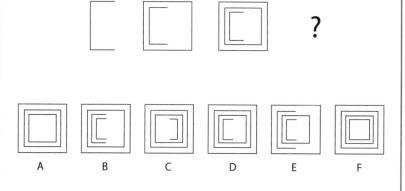

ANSWER KEY

NEXT IN LINE Squares

The answer is figure D. Squares are being built up half a square at a time, and at each new stage the left-hand half of a new inner square is added and the existing half-square is completed.

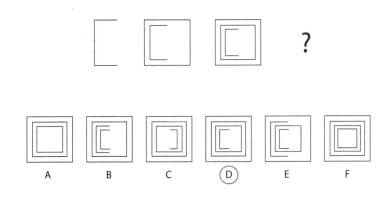

ENTANGLEMENTS

HOW TO PLAY: In the following brain teaser, you will see a layered image. Your challenge is to identify the three singular images that must be combined to create the layered image at the top.

ZOO

Answer Key

ENTANGLEMENTS Zoo

Images 6, 7, and 9 create the layered image at the top.

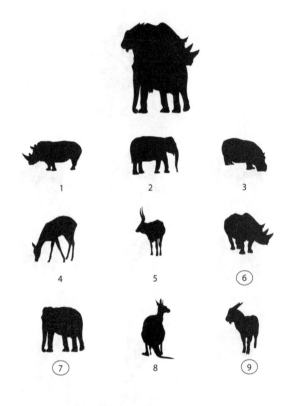

NEXT IN LINE

HOW TO PLAY: In this exercise, your right-brain challenge is to identify the figure that would logically complete the sequence. The key to the sequence is in the visual pattern. In each sequence, there is a "rule" that orders the pattern.

STAR PATTERN

ANSWER KEY

NEXT IN LINE Star Pattern

The answer is C. The two balls are following the broad path that is necessary to create the star if you were to do so without taking your pen off the paper. The next logical stop for the first ball is the bottom right tip. The second ball moves to the position the first ball just left.

HOW TO PLAY: In this exercise, your right-brain challenge is to identify the correct match or matches in response to the question posed. To do so, your right brain will need to be in high gear as you twist, turn, rotate, and flip images in your mind to find the right match.

CUBED

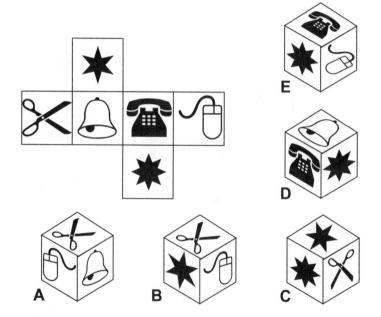

Which cube can be made from this layout?

ANSWER KEY

ROTATIONS Cubed

The answer is figure E. All of the others can be eliminated for the following reasons:

Figure A: The mouse and the bell must be on opposite sides of the cube.

Figure B: The six-pointed star is not next to the scissors' handles.

Figure C: The two stars must be on opposite sides of the cube.

Figure D: The bell is next to the phone, not above it.

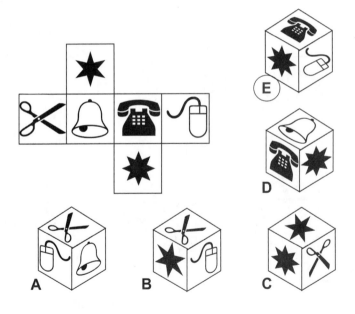

NEXT IN LINE

HOW TO PLAY: In this exercise, your right-brain challenge is to identify the figure that would logically complete the sequence. The key to the sequence is in the visual pattern. In each sequence, there is a "rule" that orders the pattern.

STICK MEN

Determine the next stick figure in the sequence.

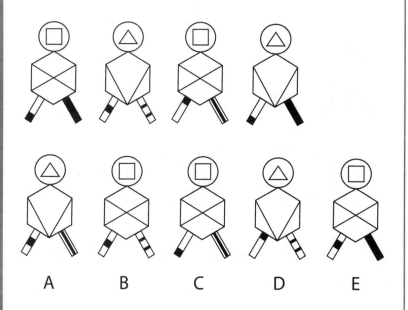

A   B   C   D   E

ANSWER KEY

NEXT IN LINE Stick Men

The answer is stick figure B. Moving across the row, the head repeats, alternating between the square and the triangle. The body repeats, alternating between between an "X" and a "V." When facing the stick figures, the left-leg black square follows a pattern of bottom, middle, top. The right-leg markings follow a pattern of solid line, horizontal stripes, vertical stripe.

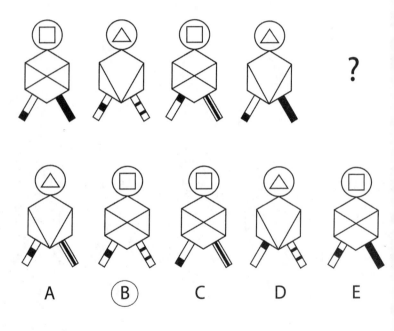

ROTATIONS

HOW TO PLAY: In this exercise, your right-brain challenge is to identify the correct match or matches in response to the question posed. To do so, your right brain will need to be in high gear as you twist, turn, rotate, and flip images in your mind to find the right match.

DOMINO THEORY

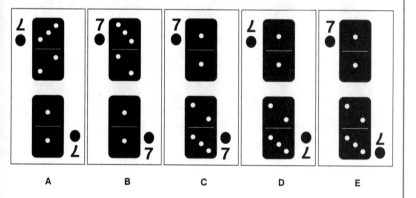

A   B   C   D   E

Find the two identical domino cards.

ANSWER KEY

ROTATIONS Domino Theory

The answer is B and D. The domino card in D has been rotated.

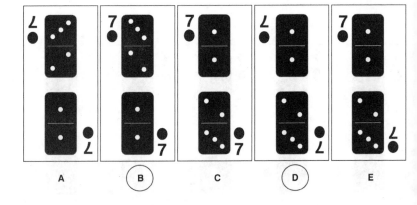

A　　B　　C　　D　　E

TURNOVER

HOW TO PLAY: The diagram on the left has been turned upside down to make the diagram on the right, but some mistakes were made. How many errors can you find?

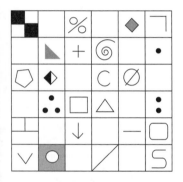

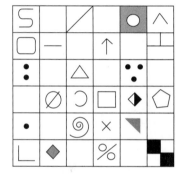

ANSWER KEY

TURN-OVER

Row 2: The + is rotated to form an X.

Row 3: The square is inserted.

Row 4, first block: The triangle has not been turned upside down.

Row 4: The rectangle is missing.

Row 5: The image has not been turned upside down.

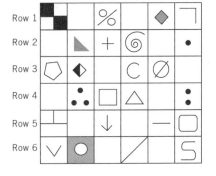

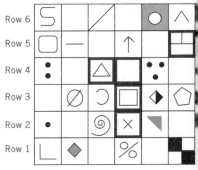

NEXT IN LINE

HOW TO PLAY: In this exercise, your right-brain challenge is to identify the figure that would logically complete the sequence. The key to the sequence is in the visual pattern. In each sequence, there is a "rule" that orders the pattern.

WHAT'S YOUR POINT?
Determine the final punctuation mark in the sequence.

?!/( )   !/( ):   /( ): --   ( ): -- _?_

?	/	"	!
A	B	C	D

NEXT IN LINE What's Your Point?

The answer is C. Each figure starts with the second punctuation mark of the previous figure. Each ends with an entirely new punctuation mark. The C response is the only new punctuation mark that could be added to the sequence; the other three have been used in the three preceding figures.

?!/( )   !/( ):   /( ): --   ( ): --<u>?</u>

?   /   "   !

A   B   (C)   D

ROTATIONS

HOW TO PLAY: In this exercise, your right-brain challenge is to identify the correct match or matches in response to the question posed. To do so, your right brain will need to be in high gear as you twist, turn, rotate, and flip images in your mind to find the right match.

FLIP-FLOP

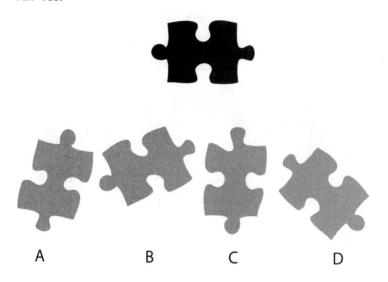

A   B   C   D

Which jigsaw-puzzle piece is the flip side of the black piece at the top?

A   B   C   D

NEXT IN LINE

HOW TO PLAY: In this exercise, your right-brain challenge is to identify the figure that would logically complete the sequence. The key to the sequence is in the visual pattern. In each sequence, there is a "rule" that orders the pattern.

ROCKAWAY

Determine the next circle in the sequence.

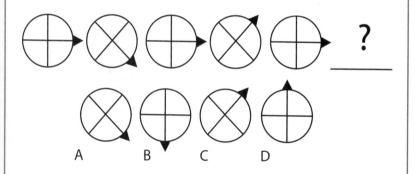

ANSWER KEY

NEXT IN LINE Rockaway

The answer is figure A. Paying attention to the title and using the concept of rocking, we can perceive that the circle is rocking. The arrow starts in the center, rocks down one line, rocks back to the center, rocks up one line, and then rocks back to the center. If the sequence continues this "rock down, rock up" pattern, the correct answer will be the arrow rocking one line down from the center again.

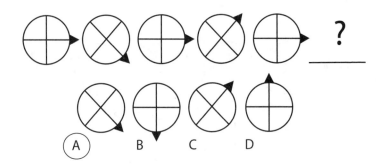

ROTATIONS

HOW TO PLAY: In this exercise, your right-brain challenge is to identify the correct match or matches in response to the question posed. To do so, your right brain will need to be in high gear as you twist, turn, rotate, and flip images in your mind to find the right match.

BLOCKED OUT

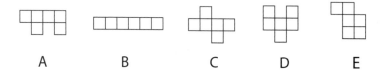

A   B   C   D   E

Which of the above layouts will form a cube?

ROTATIONS Blocked Out

The answer is figure C.

Figure A has two bottoms and no top.

Figure B has no top or bottom, only faces that will overlap.

Figure D has two tops.

Figure E cannot be bent into a cube.

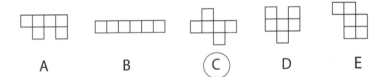

A   B   C   D   E

NEXT IN LINE

HOW TO PLAY: In this exercise, your right-brain challenge is to identify the figure that would logically complete the sequence. The key to the sequence is in the visual pattern. In each sequence, there is a "rule" that orders the pattern.

STAR AND SCROLL

Determine the next scroll in the sequence.

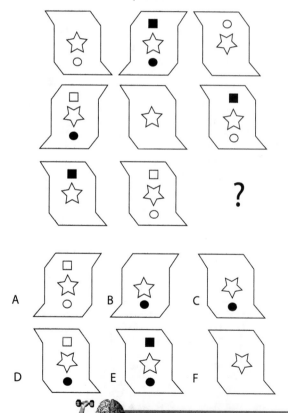

NEXT IN LINE Star and Scroll

The answer is figure B. Each row and column contains three stars, one of which is slightly rotated. Each row and column contains two white shapes and two black shapes.

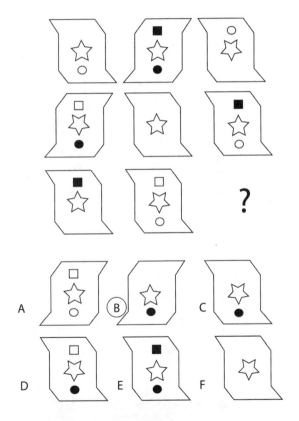

PART 3:
WHOLE BRAIN

CAN YOU THINK IT?

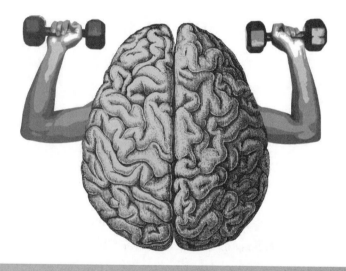

INTUITIVE-THINKING EXERCISES

Whole Brain: Can You Think It?
Intuitive-Thinking Exercises

INTRODUCTION:
The focus of the exercises in this section is on whole-brain thinking. In this workout, you'll draw on your left brain's analytical processes and your right brain's creative-intuitive processes to solve the puzzles using "out of the box" thinking.

LEFT   RIGHT

LEFT	RIGHT
Logic	Creativity
Analysis	Imagination
Sequencing	Holistic Thinking
Linear Reasoning	Intuition
Mathematics	Arts
Language	Rhythm
Facts	Nonverbal Communication
Thinking in Words	Visualization
Words of Songs	Daydreaming
Computation	Tunes of Songs
	Feelings

SEQUENCE SOLVER

HOW TO PLAY: Figure out the relationship among the items in the sequence. Then identify the item that would come next in the sequence. Look at the example below.

S, M, T, W, T, F, ___

The last letter to complete the sequence is "S." Do you know why? That's right. The letters represent the days of the week. The next day in the sequence is Saturday.

WORDS & PHRASES

1. Argentina, Bolivia, Brazil, Chile, Columbia, _____

2. octagon, heptagon, hexagon, pentagon, _____

3. Wyoming, Wisconsin, West Virginia, Washington, Virginia, _____

4. Martin Luther King Day, Presidents' Day, Memorial Day, _____

5. touchdown with 2-point conversion, touchdown with 1-point conversion, touchdown with no conversion, field goal, _____

6. April, August, December, February, January, July, June, _____

7. say, you, by, dawn's, light, _____

8. Obama, Clinton, Reagan, Ford, _____

9. sun, ray, moon, _____

10. Every, Good, Boy, Does, _____

ANSWER KEY

SEQUENCE SOLVER Words & Phrases

1. Ecuador (South American countries, in alphabetical order)

2. square (names of shapes based on number of sides in decreasing order)

3. Vermont (states in the U.S., in reverse alphabetical order)

4. Independence Day (national holidays, in sequential order)

5. 2-point safety (football points that can be scored, in reverse order)

6. March (months of the year, in alphabetical order)

7. "so" (lyrics to the American national anthem, skipping every other word)

8. Nixon (presidents in reverse order of their administrations, skipping every other president)

9. beam (sun is to ray as moon is to beam)

10. Fine (final word of the mnemonic for the lines of the treble-clef notes)

REBUS RIDDLES

HOW TO PLAY: A "rebus" is a pictorial representation of a name, word, or common phrase. To solve the following rebus puzzle, you must combine your visual and verbal perceptions to lead you to a creative answer. The example below illustrates how the thought process works. In this example, the word "head" is placed over the word "heels." The black line represents the over/under relationship. Put the visual and verbal clues together and you get the common expression below.

HEAD
———— = *HEAD OVER HEELS*
HEELS

BUSINESS SENSE

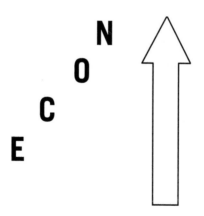

ANSWER KEY

REBUS RIDDLES Business Sense

growing economy

AHA! PUZZLES

HOW TO PLAY: AHA! puzzles are those frustrating and challenging puzzles with answers that seem "obvious" — after you solve them. However, in order to get to the obvious answer, your brain needs to do some complex parallel processing that synthesizes input from both the left- and right-brain hemispheres. Solving AHA! puzzles requires creative thinking, and the answers often come in a flash of awareness. You cannot simply "think" the solutions to these puzzles in a traditional sense. Rather, you will need to draw on both logic and visual perception.

CLIFF-HANGER

This year the owl has very wisely decided to go to sea in a beautiful luxury liner, while the pussycat has chosen to stay behind on dry land and wave good-bye from a nearby cliff top because, being a cat, she doesn't like water all that much. She looks sad because the ship is sailing perilously close to the rocky shore, and she doesn't know what to do to warn it. Quickly now! Take away six straight lines from the pussycat to avert a potential cat-astrophe!

ANSWER KEY

AHA! PUZZLES Cliff-Hanger

Take away the six lines that make up the pussycat's eyes and ears, to leave a lighthouse radiating light.

WHAT'S MY HOBBY

HOW TO PLAY: You will be presented with six sets of words. The words in each set provide clues to a hobby. Your challenge is to use the clue words to guess the hobby for each set.

Set One
guy line
billycan
bivy sack
lean-to

Set Two
tackle box
lead fly
casting
night crawler

Set Three
bench dog
bevel cut
butt joint
cross cut

Set Four
block
fusible web
patchwork
sashing

Set Five
bulb
compost
germinate
grafting

Set Six
penny black
coil
freak
commemorative

ANSWER KEY

WHAT'S MY HOBBY?

Set One: camping

Set Two: fishing

Set Three: woodworking

Set Four: quilting

Set Five: gardening

Set Six: stamp collecting

REBUS RIDDLES

HOW TO PLAY: A "rebus" is a pictorial representation of a name, word, or common phrase. To solve the following rebus puzzle, you must combine your visual and verbal perceptions to lead you to a creative answer. The example below illustrates how the thought process works. In this example, the word "head" is placed over the word "heels." The black line represents the over/under relationship. Put the visual and verbal clues together and you get the common expression below.

HEAD

――――― = HEAD OVER HEELS

HEELS

SURPRISE!

J   A   C   K

ANSWER KEY

REBUS RIDDLES Surprise!

jack-in-the-box

MINI-MYSTERIES

HOW TO PLAY: Each of the three riddles that follow contains a concealed truth. Solve the riddle and find the truth. Riddles are not difficult to solve if you use your imagination and trust your intuition. Often the truths hidden in the riddles are quite simple and just require a little "out of the box" thinking.

1. Seventy-eight students are going on a field trip to the Museum of Ancient History. The school rents a big tour bus for the event. The bus holds 79 people, including the bus driver. Why are there not enough seats on the day of the event?

2. People are gathered at night in front of their neighbors' homes. They are all ages and are holding sheets of paper in their hands. They spend a few minutes in front of each house after the homeowner comes to the door. They do not hand out the paper, and sometimes the homeowner joins them in going to the next house. Who are these people?

3. Susan comes home late for dinner to find an angry partner who says he's been waiting with food on the table for three hours. Salad, soup, and bread are sitting on a table with tall candles burning brightly. How does Susan know that her husband is exaggerating how long he's been waiting?

ANSWER KEY

MINI-MYSTERIES

1. No seat for the teacher

2. Christmas carolers

3. The candles are barely burned down.

SMALL TO BIG

HOW TO PLAY: Link the following items from small to big by drawing a continuous connecting line, starting with the smallest item and ending with the largest. Once you start, you cannot go back. If you think you made an error, just continue. You still have a chance to get most of them right. Before you begin, identify the first and last items in the sequence.

1. berry

2. snowman

3. pineapple

4. chipmunk

5. grape

6. rabbit

7. grain of sand

8. fox

9. toddler

10. kitten

11. lemon

12. ladybug

13. bear

Answer Key

SMALL TO BIG

1. grain of sand
2. ladybug
3. berry
4. grape
5. lemon
6. chipmunk
7. kitten
8. pineapple
9. rabbit
10. fox
11. toddler
12. snowman
13. bear

AHA! PUZZLES

HOW TO PLAY: AHA! puzzles are those frustrating and challenging puzzles with answers that seem "obvious" — after you solve them. However, in order to get to the obvious answer, your brain needs to do some complex parallel processing that synthesizes input from both the left- and right-brain hemispheres. Solving AHA! puzzles requires creative thinking, and the answers often come in a flash of awareness. You cannot simply "think" the solutions to these puzzles in a traditional sense. Rather, you will need to draw on both logic and visual perception.

SHIP AHOY!
This pirate ship is anchored just off a harbor. What single thing is physically impossible in this picture?

ANSWER KEY

AHA! PUZZLES Ship Ahoy!

The sails would never be up on an anchored boat.

WHAT AM I?

HOW TO PLAY: In this game, you will be presented with three sets of five clues each. The sets of clues represent characteristics of an object or a type of person. You must put the clues together to identify the person or thing each set describes.

Here is an example:

Clues: *short, green, blade, roots, yard*
Answer: *grass*

Write your answer below each set.

Set One
cold
wet
solid
slippery
translucent

Answer:

Set Two
round
fuzzy
yellow
canned
court

Answer:

Set Three
tissues
sleep
soup
sneeze
fever

Answer:

ANSWER KEY

WHAT AM I?

Set One: ice

Set Two: tennis ball

Set Three: flu

PICTURE PASTE

HOW TO PLAY: In this game, you will be presented with two boxes of words side by side. Your brain challenge is to arrange one word from each side to form a recognizable compound word. For example, the word combos "car wheel" and "kitchen chair" would lead you to the compound word "wheelchair." If you are artistically inclined and right-brain dominant, you might find it helpful to draw a quick sketch of possible images that the word combos might form.

playing card: club suit	house arrest

fourth quarter	person's back

human tooth	miner's pick

pile of clothes	horse farm

daily run	one way

fiscal year	black book

ANSWER KEY

PICTURE PASTE

1. clubhouse
2. quarterback
3. toothpick
4. clotheshorse
5. runway
6. yearbook

REBUS RIDDLES

HOW TO PLAY: A "rebus" is a pictorial representation of a name, word, or common phrase. To solve the following rebus puzzle, you must combine your visual and verbal perceptions to lead you to a creative answer. The example below illustrates how the thought process works. In this example, the word "head" is placed over the word "heels." The black line represents the over/under relationship. Put the visual and verbal clues together and you get the common expression below.

HEAD
—————— = *HEAD OVER HEELS*
HEELS

DANGER!

COVER

COVER   HEAD   COVER

COVER

Answer Key

REBUS RIDDLES Danger!

head for cover

AHA! PUZZLES

HOW TO PLAY: AHA! puzzles are those frustrating and challenging puzzles with answers that seem "obvious" — after you solve them. However, in order to get to the obvious answer, your brain needs to do some complex parallel processing that synthesizes input from both the left- and right-brain hemispheres. Solving AHA! puzzles requires creative thinking, and the answers often come in a flash of awareness. You cannot simply "think" the solutions to these puzzles in a traditional sense. Rather, you will need to draw on both logic and visual perception.

COSMIC, MAN!
Can you add the three objects from the far right to the space scene on the left to start a cosmic meltdown? You may place them behind those already in the picture.

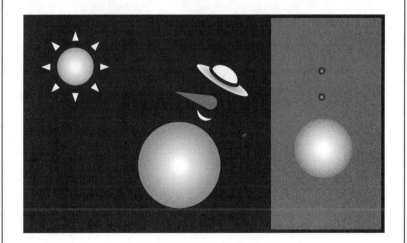

ANSWER KEY

AHA! PUZZLES Cosmic, Man!

Add the objects as indicated to create a snowman.

WHAT'S MY HOBBY?

HOW TO PLAY: In this game, you will be presented with six sets of four clues each. Your challenge is to use the clue words to guess the hobby for each set.

Set One
aperture
cropping
exposure
negative

Set Two
bind off
purl
cast on
needle

Set Three
cleat
dead ahead
stern
wake

Set Four
belay
edging
bouldering
rappel

Set Five
bonk
bunny hop
chain suck
downshift

Set Six
back tack
baste marking
notches
sizing

ANSWER KEY

WHAT'S MY HOBBY?

Set One: photography

Set Two: knitting

Set Three: boating

Set Four: mountain climbing

Set Five: cycling

Set Six: sewing

WORD FORMULAS

HOW TO PLAY: In the following exercise, each group of numbers and letters combines to form a familiar statement. See how quickly you can find the solution to the word formula. For example:

Word Formula: 5 = N. of P. on a B. T.

Solution: 5 = number of players on a basketball team

a. 12 = E. in a D.

b. 52 = W. in a Y.

c. 5 = F. on a H.

d. 4 = Q. in a D.

e. 26 = L. in the A.

f. 8 = P. in the S. S.

g. 52 = P.C. in a D.

h. 8 = O. in a C.

ANSWER KEY

WORD FORMULAS

a. eggs in a dozen

b. weeks in a year

c. fingers on a hand

d. quarters in a dollar

e. letters in the alphabet

f. planets in the solar system

g. playing cards in a deck

h. ounces in a cup

TAKE IT AWAY

HOW TO PLAY: In the following four sets, you will be presented with lists containing three items each. One of the items does not belong in the list, because it differs in some fundamental way from the remaining two items. Your job is to find and circle the "odd one out" in each set. Here's an example:

Maltese, poodle, spaniel

While all of these are dogs, you would circle spaniel. Do you know why? That's right — a spaniel has dog fur, while the other two breeds have nonallergenic "real" hair.

Set One
Siamese
Maltese
Bernese

Set Two
Memorial Day
Labor Day
Halloween

Set Three
cirrus
sedimentary
cumulonimbus

Set Four
furnace
volcano
tea kettle

ANSWER KEY

TAKE IT AWAY

Set One: Siamese (Maltese and Bernese are dogs.)

Set Two: Halloween (Memorial Day and Labor Day are national holidays.)

Set Three: sedimentary (Cirrus and cumulonimbus are types of clouds.)

Set Four: furnace (A volcano and a tea kettle "blow their tops.")

AHA! PUZZLES

HOW TO PLAY: AHA! puzzles are those frustrating and challenging puzzles with answers that seem "obvious" — after you solve them. However, in order to get to the obvious answer, your brain needs to do some complex parallel processing that synthesizes input from both the left- and right-brain hemispheres. Solving AHA! puzzles requires creative thinking, and the answers often come in a flash of awareness. You cannot simply "think" the solutions to these puzzles in a traditional sense. Rather, you will need to draw on both logic and visual perception.

PARLEZ-VOUS FRANÇAIS?
You are at a garden party hosted by the Count and Countess de Vine at Le Chateau Bordeaux. Go on, don't be shy. Even though you may not speak French very well, raise a glass and try to make some kind of "chat."

ANSWER KEY

AHA! PUZZLES Parlez-Vous Français?

In French, the word "chat" means cat, so just raise the glass in the picture to create this cat face.

WHAT AM I?

How to Play: In this game, you will be presented with three sets of five clues each. The sets of clues represent characteristics of an object or a type of person. You must put the clues together to identify the person or thing each set describes.

Here is an example:

Clues: *short, green, blade, roots, yard*
Answer: *grass*

Write your answer below each set.

Set One
spouse
summons
custody
judge
court

Answer:

Set Two
small
swallow
daily
health
C, D, E

Answer:

Set Three
stone
inherit
royal
cold
edifice

Answer:

ANSWER KEY

WHAT AM I?

Set One: divorce

Set Two: vitamin

Set Three: castle

REBUS RIDDLES

HOW TO PLAY: A "rebus" is a pictorial representation of a name, word, or common phrase. To solve the following rebus puzzle, you must combine your visual and verbal perceptions to lead you to a creative answer. The example below illustrates how the thought process works. In this example, the word "head" is placed over the word "heels." The black line represents the over/under relationship. Put the visual and verbal clues together and you get the common expression below.

HEAD
─────── = *HEAD OVER HEELS*
HEELS

LOOKING TIRED

HIS iiiiiiiii
─────────────────
O   O   O   O

ANSWER KEY

REBUS RIDDLES Looking Tired

circles under his eyes

SEQUENCE SOLVER

HOW TO PLAY: Figure out the relationship among the items in the sequence. Then identify the item that would come next in the sequence. Look at the example below.

say, you, by, dawn's, light _____

The last word to complete the sequence is "so." Do you know why? That's right. The words represent the opening lyrics from "The Star-Spangled Banner," with every other word missing from the lyrics.

1. b, f, j, n, r, _____

2. elephant, camel, lion, dog, _____

3. u, o, i, e, _____

4. diamond, emerald, pearl, ruby, peridot, _____

5. ace, eight, five, four, jack, _____

6. Alabama, Alaska, California, Colorado, Delaware, Florida, Georgia, _____

7. kindergarten, middle school, high school, bachelor, master's, _____

8. bronze, silver, gold, _____

9. aqua, crimson, emerald, green, _____

10. Biden, Cheney, Gore, Quayle, _____

11. 46, 40, 39, 33, 32, 26, _____

12. love, 15, 30, 40, _____

13. frog, tadpole, _____

14. J, O, P, Q, R, _____

15. double bogey, bogey, par, _____

ANSWER KEY

SEQUENCE SOLVER

1. v (increase by 4 letters)
2. any mammal smaller than a dog (decreasing by size)
3. a (vowels in reverse order)
4. sapphire (birthstones, in order of months)
5. king (playing cards, by first-letter alphabetical order)
6. Hawaii (U.S. states in alphabetical order, by first letter of state)
7. Ph.D. (advancing academic degrees)
8. platinum (metals by increasing industrial worth)
9. ivory or indigo (names of colors in alphabetical order, skipping every other letter)
10. Bush (vice presidents in reverse order)
11. 25 (pattern is subtract by 6, subtract by 1, and repeat)
12. game (tennis points, with scores in increasing value)
13. egg (life cycle of a frog in reverse order)
14. S (increasing capital letters of the alphabet that are formed using rounded lines)
15. birdie (golf scores per hole, by decreasing number of strokes)

PALINDROMES

HOW TO PLAY: A "palindrome" is a word, phrase, verse, or sentence that reads the same backward or forward. In this game, you will be given a clue for a one-word palindrome. Your challenge is to use the clue to identify the palindrome, as in the example below.

Clue: A call for help.

Answer: SOS

1. an explosive device

2. a baby barnyard-animal sound

3. Adam's significant other

4. male and female genders

5. a sound made by a train

6. a small child

7. the opposite of "bro"

8. an expression of surprise or delight

9. Mario Andretti drives one

10. what you look through

11. a type of boat for rowing on water

12. how you address a married Frenchwoman

13. midday

14. a type of rally held before a school sporting event, like football or basketball

15. a female sheep

ANSWER KEY

PALINDROMES

1. TNT
2. peep
3. Eve
4. sexes
5. toot
6. tot
7. sis
8. wow
9. race car
10. eye
11. kayak
12. madam
13. noon
14. pep
15. ewe

AHA! PUZZLES

HOW TO PLAY: AHA! puzzles are those frustrating and challenging puzzles with answers that seem "obvious" — after you solve them. However, in order to get to the obvious answer, your brain needs to do some complex parallel processing that synthesizes input from both the left- and right-brain hemispheres. Solving AHA! puzzles requires creative thinking, and the answers often come in a flash of awareness. You cannot simply "think" the solutions to these puzzles in a traditional sense. Rather, you will need to draw on both logic and visual perception.

SUITED UP

As you can see, Biscuit the Clown is wearing a very snazzy suit. His favorite party trick is to change out of it into another suit at the drop of a hat. What does this other suit look like?

ANSWER KEY

AHA! PUZZLES Suited Up

Drop the hat to the bottom of the picture, color Biscuit's suit black, and you have the representation of the card suit — spades.

MINI-MYSTERIES

HOW TO PLAY: Each of the three sets of riddles that follow contains a concealed truth. Solve the riddle and find the truth. Riddles are not difficult to solve if you use your imagination and trust your intuition. Often the truths hidden in riddles are quite simple and just require a little "out of the box" thinking.

1. Elizabeth is taking a class at a local community college in her spare time. She's given a vocabulary sheet full of terms like "meter," "time," "3/4", "clef," and "scale." What is she learning about?

2. Little Jolee goes to visit Grandma in Florida. When she gets home her Mom asks her what she did with Grandma. Jolee says they walked around strangers' lawns looking for old toys. What were Jolee and Grandma doing?

3. Dan is looking for milk in the refrigerator. He sees milk in a plastic container, but he doesn't drink it. He tells his wife that they are out of milk. She comes into the kitchen carrying the baby. She looks in the refrigerator and agrees that they are out of milk. She says she'll pick some up today. How is this possible?

ANSWER KEY

MINI-MYSTERIES

1. music theory

2. They were going to yard sales.

3. The refrigerated milk is breast milk for the baby.

TAKE IT AWAY

HOW TO PLAY: In the following four sets, you will be presented with lists containing three items each. One of the items does not belong in the list, because it differs in some fundamental way from the remaining two items. Your job is to find and circle the "odd one out" in each set. Here's an example:

Maltese, poodle, spaniel

While all of these are dogs, you would circle spaniel. Do you know why? That's right — a spaniel has dog fur, while the other two breeds have nonallergenic "real" hair.

Set Five
doorbell
door knocker
doorknob

Set Six
rickshaw
bicycle
car

Set Seven
frigid
tepid
scorching

Set Eight
John Quincy Adams
Franklin D. Roosevelt
George W. Bush

Answer Key

TAKE IT AWAY

Set Five: doorknob (A doorbell and a door knocker make a sound.)

Set Six: car (A rickshaw and a bicycle have two wheels.)

Set Seven: frigid (Tepid and scorching are degrees of warmth.)

Set Eight: Franklin D. Roosevelt (John Quincy Adams and George W. Bush had fathers who were presidents, too.)

REBUS RIDDLES

HOW TO PLAY: A "rebus" is a pictorial representation of a name, word, or common phrase. To solve the following rebus puzzle, you must combine your visual and verbal perceptions to lead you to a creative answer. The example below illustrates how the thought process works. In this example, the word "head" is placed over the word "heels." The black line represents the over/under relationship. Put the visual and verbal clues together and you get the common expression below.

HEAD
——— = *HEAD OVER HEELS*
HEELS

GIVE AWAY

Grab

Grab

Grab

Grab

ANSWER KEY

REBUS RIDDLES Give Away

up for grabs

RHYME MAKER

HOW TO PLAY: Each of the following phrases can be translated into a rhyming pair of words. For example the combination "pallid man" can become the rhyming pair "pale male."

NATURAL KINGDOM

Phrases Rare	Rhyming Pair
1. Black Sea predator	
2. obese rodent	
3. comical hare	
4. swine toupee	

Answer Key

RHYME MAKER Natural Kingdom

1. dark shark
2. fat rat
3. funny bunny
4. pig wig

MINI-MYSTERIES

HOW TO PLAY: Each of the two riddles that follow contain a concealed truth. Solve the riddle and find the truth. Riddles are not difficult to solve if you use your imagination and trust your intuition. Often the truths hidden in riddles are qsuite simple and just require a little "out of the box" thinking.

AT THE BALLET
Brian is eating his favorite health-food snack. In order to eat it, he needs a special tool. When he thinks of this tool, he often thinks of his favorite ballet. What is the name of the tool?

AT THE RESTAURANT
Gracie is in a fine restaurant. Everyone around her is eating and drinking. Gracie is carrying a glass of wine in her hand. Although she enjoys a glass of wine from time to time, she will not take one sip tonight. What is Gracie doing?

ANSWER KEY

MINI-MYSTERIES

At the Ballet
nutcracker

At the Restaurant
cocktail waitressing

AHA! PUZZLES

HOW TO PLAY: AHA! puzzles are those frustrating and challenging puzzles with answers that seem "obvious" — *after* you solve them. However, in order to get to the obvious answer, your brain needs to do some complex parallel processing that synthesizes input from both the left- and right-brain hemispheres. Solving AHA! puzzles requires creative thinking, and the answers often come in a flash of awareness. You cannot simply "think" the solutions to these puzzles in a traditional sense. Rather, you will need to draw on both logic and visual perception.

TEMPERATURE READING

Is this mug of coffee warm, lukewarm, or cool, and how do you know?

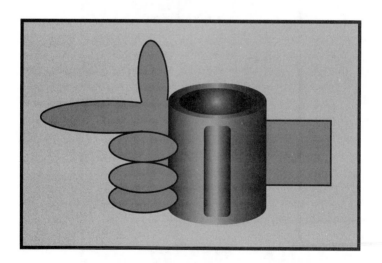

ANSWER KEY

AHA! PUZZLES Temperature Reading

The coffee is cool. Mentally flip the image so that the fingers are on the top. The fingers holding the cup now spell out the word "cool."

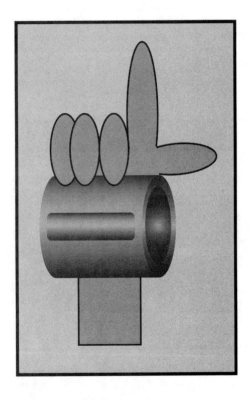

FILL IN THE PUN

HOW TO PLAY: A *pun* is a form of wordplay that suggests two or more meanings, by exploiting multiple meanings of words, or of similar-sounding words, for an intended humorous or rhetorical effect. Here are three examples of puns. The pun (word with the double meaning) is in italics.

1. He has been a jogger for three years *running.*

2. An electrician's work is well *grounded.*

3. He had a difficult time *bouncing* back from his bungee-cord accident.

In this brain challenge, you will be given a sentence and asked to fill in the pun. The puzzle title provides a clue to the pun.

BODY PART
The butcher backed into the meat grinder and got a little _____ in his work.

BOOTLEGGER
She was only a backwoods whiskey maker, but he loved her

_____.

FILL IN THE PUN

Body Part

behind

Bootlegger

still

REBUS RIDDLES

HOW TO PLAY: A "rebus" is a pictorial representation of a name, word, or common phrase. To solve the following rebus puzzle, you must combine your visual and verbal perceptions to lead you to a creative answer. The example below illustrates how the thought process works. In this example, the word "head" is placed over the word "heels." The black line represents the over/under relationship. Put the visual and verbal clues together and you get the common expression below.

HEAD
——— = *HEAD OVER HEELS*
HEELS

CROWD CONTROL

1

10   2

9   3

        S A F E T Y

8   4

7   5

        6

ANSWER KEY

REBUS RIDDLES Crowd Control

safety in numbers

AHA! PUZZLES

HOW TO PLAY: AHA! puzzles are those frustrating and challenging puzzles with answers that seem "obvious" — *after* you solve them. However, in order to get to the obvious answer, your brain needs to do some complex parallel processing that synthesizes input from both the left- and right-brain hemispheres. Solving AHA! puzzles requires creative thinking, and the answers often come in a flash of awareness. You cannot simply "think" the solutions to these puzzles in a traditional sense. Rather, you will need to draw on both logic and visual perception.

CINDERSPELLER

What animal's name has been used to create this demonic-looking cat with a forked tail?

AHA! PUZZLES Cinderspeller

A mouse. The shapes (starting with the ears, then moving down and over to the tail) spell out M–O–U–S–E.

MINI-MYSTERIES

HOW TO PLAY: Each of the two riddles that follow contain a concealed truth. Solve the riddle and find the truth. Riddles are not difficult to solve if you use your imagination and trust your intuition. Often the truths hidden in riddles are qsuite simple and just require a little "out of the box" thinking.

AT HOME

Lucy owns a house, but she only uses it during the winter-holiday season. While she admires it from the outside, she never steps inside. At the end of the season the house is gone, only to be rebuilt again next year. She is not a carpenter. Her houses always have a wonderful smell, but she doesn't use air fresheners. What kind of a house is it?

AT AN EVENT

Julia puts on a disguise and heads out for the evening. She goes to a building filled with people and seats. Everyone is facing a large screen. She sits there for about 2 hours, during which she sees her own image many times over on the screen. Afterwards, she sneaks out so she will not be recognized by the crowd. Who is Julia?

Answer Key

MINI-MYSTERIES

At Home
gingerbread house

At an Event
an actress in the film

FILL IN THE PUN

HOW TO PLAY: A *pun* is a form of wordplay that suggests two or more meanings, by exploiting multiple meanings of words, or of similar-sounding words, for an intended humorous or rhetorical effect. Here are three examples of puns. The pun (word with the double meaning) is in italics.

1. He has been a jogger for three years *running*.

2. An electrician's work is well *grounded*.

3. He had a difficult time *bouncing* back from his bungee-cord accident.

In this brain challenge, you will be given a sentence and asked to fill in the pun. The puzzle title provides a clue to the pun.

MEN'S APPAREL
Two silkworms had a race. They ended up in a _____.

HAT TRICK
Two hats were hanging on a hat rack in the hallway. One hat said to the other, "You should stay here. I'll go on _____ _____."

Answer Key

FILL IN THE PUN

Men's Apparel

tie

Hat Trick

a head

REBUS RIDDLES

HOW TO PLAY: A "rebus" is a pictorial representation of a name, word, or common phrase. To solve the following rebus puzzle, you must combine your visual and verbal perceptions to lead you to a creative answer. The example below illustrates how the thought process works. In this example, the word "head" is placed over the word "heels." The black line represents the over/under relationship. Put the visual and verbal clues together and you get the common expression below.

HEAD
——— = HEAD OVER HEELS
HEELS

PUSHING DAISIES

G R O U N D

FEET	**FEET**
FEET	**FEET**
FEET	**FEET**

ANSWER KEY

REBUS RIDDLES Pushing Daisies

six feet underground

RHYME MAKER

HOW TO PLAY: Each of the following phrases can be translated into a rhyming pair of words. For example the combination "pallid man" can become the rhyming pair "pale male."

SHIP AHOY

Phrases Rare	Rhyming Pair
1. big cargo boat	
2. crazy flat boat	
3. nap on a passenger ship	

ANSWER KEY

RHYME MAKER Ship Ahoy

1. large barge
2. daft raft
3. cruise snooze

AHA! PUZZLES

HOW TO PLAY: AHA! puzzles are those frustrating and challenging puzzles with answers that seem "obvious" — *after* you solve them. However, in order to get to the obvious answer, your brain needs to do some complex parallel processing that synthesizes input from both the left- and right-brain hemispheres. Solving AHA! puzzles requires creative thinking, and the answers often come in a flash of awareness. You cannot simply "think" the solutions to these puzzles in a traditional sense. Rather, you will need to draw on both logic and visual perception.

SPOT-ON

Can you fill in the missing spot?

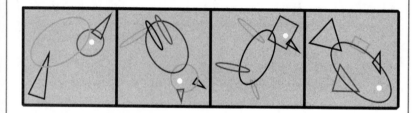

ANSWER KEY

AHA! PUZZLES Spot-On

Box 2 requires a second spot to complete the front view of the cat's two eyes.

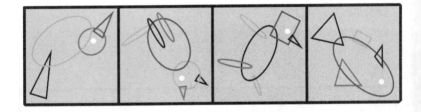

REBUS RIDDLES

HOW TO PLAY: A "rebus" is a pictorial representation of a name, word, or common phrase. To solve the following rebus puzzle, you must combine your visual and verbal perceptions to lead you to a creative answer. The example below illustrates how the thought process works. In this example, the word "head" is placed over the word "heels." The black line represents the over/under relationship. Put the visual and verbal clues together and you get the common expression below.

HEAD
——— = *HEAD OVER HEELS*
HEELS

NOT MAKING ANY HEADWAY

ANSWER KEY

REBUS RIDDLES Not Making Any Headway

running in circles

RIDDLE ME THIS

How to Play: Here are two classic riddles. Use your right brain to visualize the images described in the riddles. Use your left brain to see the logic in the images. Then answer the question, "What Am I?"

STAY DRY

To cross the water I'm the way,

For water I'm above;

I touch it not, and truth to say,

I neither swim nor move.

What am I?

ANATOMY

Two bodies have I,

Tho' both joined in one;

The stiller I stand,

The faster I run.

What am I?

ANSWER KEY

RIDDLE ME THIS

Stay Dry

a bridge

Anatomy

an hourglass

PICTURE RHYMES

HOW TO PLAY: You will be presented with a series of pictures. Each picture can be represented by two rhyming words. For example, a picture of the United States' White House could be translated into the rhyming phrase *president's residence*. In addition to the picture, you will be provided with the first initials of the two rhyming words. For *president's residence*, the initial clues would be *P-R*. For an additional challenge, cover the art clues with your hand.

FANCY BIRD — S-G

COZY SLEEPOVER — S-B

SLEEPING FLOWER — L-D

ANIMAL COMFORT — H-C

SCANDINAVIAN TRAVELER — B-V

ANSWER KEY

PICTURE RHYMES

Fancy Bird
spruced goose

Cozy Sleepover
snug bug

Sleeping Flower
lazy daisy

Animal Comfort
hare chair

Scandinavian Traveler
biking Viking

BRAINTEASERS

HOW TO PLAY: This challenge presents a mix of word, number, and symbol puzzles. See how quickly you can switch between your right brain and your left brain to solve the puzzles.

1. What common expression is represented by this rebus puzzle?

   Often

   Often   Not

   Often

   Often

2. What common expression is represented by this numeric sequence?

   1/4-1/4-1/4-1/4-1/4-1/4-1/4-1/4-1/4-1/4-1/4-1/4

3. Can you solve this math puzzle?

   Start with the number of partridges in a pear tree, add the black sheep's bags of wool, and multiply by how often something happens in a blue moon.

4. What common saying is represented by these "big" words?

   The tenderest of passions and feelings causes the rotational force propelling this inhabited planet.

5. What name doesn't belong?

   Larry, Kristy, Jane, David, Amy

6. What is at the center of Earth?

7. A camera and case cost $100. The camera costs $80 more than the case. How much does the camera cost?

8. Mr. Roberts has all birds except one, and he has all cats except one. How many birds and cats does he have?

9. What part of London is in France?

10. What U.S. state is round on both sides and high in the middle?

Whole Brain: *Can you think it?* **285**

ANSWER KEY

BRAIN TEASERS

1. more often than not

2. close quarters

3. The answer is 4 (1 partridge + 3 bags of wool = 4 x 1 in a blue moon).

4. Love makes the world go round.

5. Kristy doesn't contain the letter "a."

6. the letter "r"

7. $90

8. one bird and one cat

9. the letter "n"

10. Ohio

BUS STOP

HOW TO PLAY: This picture was shown to preschoolers and kindergartners. They were asked, "Which way is the bus going?" They got the answer right in a matter of seconds. Can you?

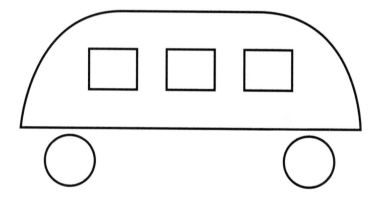

ANSWER KEY

BUS STOP

The children answered without hesitation that the bus was going to the "left." When asked why, they answered, "Because you can't see the door."

LATERAL THINKING

HOW TO PLAY: The term "lateral thinking" was coined by Dr. Edward de Bono to denote a problem-solving style that involves looking at the given situation from unexpected angles and new perspectives. Sometimes, a problem seems insoluble because our assumptions about it are wrong. Dr. de Bono explains it this way: "You cannot dig a hole in a different place by digging the same hole deeper." This means that trying harder in the same direction may not be as useful as changing direction. On the surface, lateral-thinking puzzles seem difficult, but the answers are often just a matter of using simple logic, with a dose of "out of the box" thinking.

Test your lateral-thinking skills with these classic brainteasers.

GOING UP?
There is a woman who lives on the top floor of a very tall building. Every day she takes the elevator down to the ground floor to leave the building to go to work. Upon returning from work, though, she can only travel halfway up in the elevator and has to walk the rest of the way, unless it's raining. Why?

OH, NUTS!
A man is replacing a wheel on his car when he accidentally drops the four nuts used to hold the wheel on the car, and they fall into a deep drain, irretrievably lost. A passing girl offers him a solution, which enables him to drive home. What is it?

ANSWER KEY

LATERAL THINKING

Going Up?

The woman is very, very short and can only reach halfway up the bank of elevator buttons. However, if it is raining, she will have her umbrella with her and can press the higher buttons with it.

Oh, Nuts!

Use one nut from each of the other three wheels.

AHA! PUZZLE

HOW TO PLAY: AHA! puzzles are those frustrating and challenging puzzles with answers that seem "obvious" — *after* you solve them. However, in order to get to the obvious answer, your brain needs to do some complex parallel processing that synthesizes input from both the left- and right-brain hemispheres. Solving AHA! puzzles requires creative thinking, and the answers often come in a flash of awareness. You cannot simply "think" the solutions to these puzzles in a traditional sense. Rather, you will need to draw on both logic and visual perception.

DISAPPEARING PARROT TRICK
Picture A: Polly the parrot in her cage.
Picture B: Where has Polly gone?

ANSWER KEY

AHA! PUZZLES Disapearing Parrot Trick

Polly gone? No, she became a polygon (the shape).

CONNECT THE DOTS

HOW TO PLAY: Here is a well-known whole-brain exercise. Solving the puzzle requires visualization and logic. The challenge is to link all nine dots using four (or fewer) straight lines, without lifting the pencil off the page. (If you get stuck, read the clue below to get a fresh perspective on the solution.)

Visualize a kite.

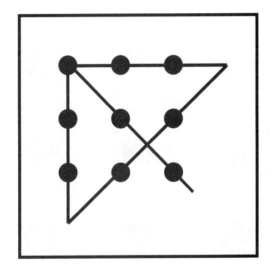

IMAGINE WHY

HOW TO PLAY: "Imagine Why" is a creative-thinking exercise that incorporates the techniques of *free association* and *stream of consciousness*. In this exercise, there are no "right" answers. The goal is to freely generate possible scenarios without restriction. Let your imagination be your guide. Generate one response for each question. Then, try a second round to see if you can come up with an alternative scenario for the same question.

1. Why is ice forming in the summer?

2. Why are the men being separated from the women?

3. Why are the animals running to high ground?

4. Why is the woman in the business suit walking barefoot on a New York City sidewalk?

5. Why is the Spanish teacher teaching English?

6. Why are manhole covers round?

7. Why do some people report multiple UFO sightings while others never see one?

8. Why is the American family driving on the wrong side of the road?

9. Why does the bicyclist ride into town on one wheel?

ANSWER KEY

IMAGINE WHY

Here are some possible scenarios. What did you guess?

1. Kids are making popsicles.

2. They are forming two opposite lines for square dancing.

3. A tidal wave is coming due to an ocean earthquake.

4. She broke her high heel in a sidewalk grate.

5. She is teaching Spanish-speaking children how to speak English.

6. So that when you take them off, they can't slip and fall through the opening.

7. People who report seeing multiple UFOs believe they exist and spend a lot of time looking up to the skies for proof.

8. They are driving on the opposite side of the road because they are in England, not the U.S.

9. Because he is riding a unicycle.

SEEING SQUARES

HOW TO PLAY: In this puzzle, you will use visualization to see the overlapping possibilities, and use logic to deduce the correct answer.

SQUARES

How many squares do you see in this 5" x 5" checkerboard?

ANSWER KEY

SEEING SQUARES Squares

There are a total of 55 squares.

There are 25 squares that are 1" x 1."

There are 16 squares that are 2" x 2."

There are 9 squares that are 3" x 3."

There are 4 squares that are 4" x 4."

There is 1 square that is 5" x 5."

REBUS RIDDLES

HOW TO PLAY: A "rebus" is a pictorial representation of a name, word, or common phrase. To solve the following rebus puzzle, you must combine your visual and verbal perceptions to lead you to a creative answer. The example below illustrates how the thought process works. In this example, the word "head" is placed over the word "heels." The black line represents the over/under relationship. Put the visual and verbal clues together and you get the common expression below.

HEAD
——— = HEAD OVER HEELS
HEELS

What is the common expression?

M 1 Y 1 L 1 F 1 E

What type of medical procedure is this?

O _ ER _ T _ O _

Answer Key

REBUS RIDDLES

once in my life

painless operation

AHA! PUZZLE

HOW TO PLAY: AHA! puzzles are those frustrating and challenging puzzles with answers that seem "obvious" — *after* you solve them. However, in order to get to the obvious answer, your brain needs to do some complex parallel processing that synthesizes input from both the left- and right-brain hemispheres. Solving AHA! puzzles requires creative thinking, and the answers often come in a flash of awareness. You cannot simply "think" the solutions to these puzzles in a traditional sense. Rather, you will need to draw on both logic and visual perception.

WHAT'S HER LINE?

Can you match each woman with her occupation, using her hairstyle as a clue? The possibilities (in no particular order) are: golfer, matchmaker, gardener, jeweler.

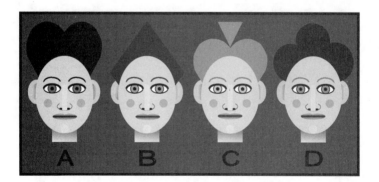

ANSWER KEY

AHA! PUZZLES What's Her Line?

A. heart = matchmaker

B. diamond = jeweler

C. spade = gardener

D. club = golfer

PLAYING WITH MATCHES

HOW TO PLAY: In this matchstick puzzle, you must move six matches to make ten.

  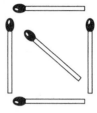

ANSWER KEY

PLAYING WITH MATCHES

By removing the six indicated matchsticks, you are left with the word "TEN."